MIGHTY BLUE JUSTICE!

MIGHTY BLUE JUSTICE!

GREG HYLAND

BERKLEY BOULEVARD BOOKS, NEW YORK

THE TICK: MIGHTY BLUE JUSTICE!

A Berkley Boulevard Book / published by arrangement with Saban Merchandising, Inc. and Saban International N.V.

PRINTING HISTORY
Berkley Boulevard trade paperback edition / May 1997

The Penguin Putnam Inc. World Wide Web site address is
http://www.penguinputnam.com

ISBN: 0-425-16705-4

BERKLEY BOULEVARD
Berkley Boulevard Books are published by The Berkley Publishing Group,
a division of Penguin Putnam Inc.,
375 Hudson Street, New York, New York 10014.
BERKLEY BOULEVARD and its logo are trademarks
belonging to Penguin Putnam Inc.

PRINTED IN THE UNITED STATES OF AMERICA

15   14   13   12   11   10

CONTENTS!

I'D LIKE TO SAY THANKS TO SOME OF THE PEOPLE
WHO HELPED ME OUT WITH THIS BOOK, THROUGH KIND
WORDS, SUPPORT AND THEFT. PLEASE HOLD YOUR
APPLAUSE UNTIL ALL THE NAMES HAVE BEEN MENTIONED:

BEN EDLUND AND CHRIS McCULLOUGH
EVAN DORKIN
STEVE REMEN, NADINE WETTLAUFER,
BRIAN LEMAY AND TRAYNOR, GREG & MARGARET
ALEXANDER
AND MOST OF ALL
BARRY NEVILLE, RICHARD SILLETT
AND JILL DINNEEN

-GREG HYLAND

PART 1: MEET THE TICK!

WELCOME TO MY BOOK. ISN'T IT KEEN?
BY *THE TICK*

Greetings, citizens of the world. I am The Tick. GET TO KNOW ME!

And that's exactly what will happen as your eyes scan over the words found within the very pages you now hold. Over the years, working as The City's leaping blue protector, and encountering villainy of all shapes and smells, I have kept a Secret Tick Notebook.

But this notebook is secret no more, no!

In an effort to educate, inform, and guide young minds, I have given one lucky little publishing company the exclusive right to reprint all that my shocking notebook contains, bind it in a convenient and pleasing form, distribute it to the bookstores of the world, and sell it to you. It's shocking and amazing! It's all here for you, gentle reader: Mighty Blue Justice!

Mighty, for I am mighty! Mighty like the salmon fighting the strong currents of a river he once called home. Blue, for I am blue! Blue like a summer sky so clear you see little floaty lights in your eyes as you lie on the grass looking up. And Justice, for I AM JUSTICE! Like a weird blue icicle that hangs off the world's awning and drips molten mercy and good deeds upon the meek and kind, while always ready to detach and plunge into the foul headbone of a particularly bad person.

There are many books in this wonderful world; some are about the animals in the Chinese Zodiac, how to get water out of a cactus, hydroelectric power, the Ottoman Empire, or even the centuries-old secrets of Ninjitsu. But none are about me!

Until now.

MEET THE TICK!

Prepare, fair reader, to learn everything that you need to know about me, The Tick!

And Arthur. Yes, Arthur, too. So now you will learn everything there is to know about me and Arthur. Me and Arthur and the other fine members of The City's crime fighting community. Yes, they're in here, too. So, in review, you will find encased between these very covers all you could need to know about me, The Tick; loyal doughy Arthur; and respected colleagues like American Maid, Die Fledermaus, Sewer Urchin, Crusading Chameleon, The Civic Minded Five, and, yes, even the Human Bullet.

And villains. Villains are here, too. Without their hideous and twisted brains, who would I battle? You can read about those who stood up for badness. But remember, when the whole class is sitting there and someone stands up and says "I wanna be evil!" who will make 'em stand in the corner and wear the dunce cap of justice? I'll tell you who! The Tick! So learn of all my terrible foes, and when you do, remember, just don't hold the book too close to your face!

I've also provided stunning information about how you, the loyal book-buying public, can do your duty and become a superhero, just like me! You'll learn how to turn your apartment or guest room into a pulsating super-crime-busting headquarters, make a multi-transforming vehicle, develop a super-persona, and gather an evil-stopping arsenal. And I'll even help you devise a nifty battle cry. It's all here. I'm tingly with delight, just thinking about it! Aren't you?

Your shaking hands probably can't wait to turn the pages to find all that is contained within. And I can't blame your impatience. So, enough from me, for now, chum. Get reading!

-THE TICK

MIGHTY BLUE JUSTICE!

INTERVIEWS!

It seems the public has an insatiable appetite for information on those of us in the fabulous superhero community. And can you blame them? Magazines write about us! Television shows shows about us! It's all terribly exciting. Here is a collection of magazine articles, interviews, and notes that I've gathered, or, rather, ARCHIVED, for super-important reference and research purposes. And some of them are even about me! Keen!

Question: Once again, we are here with prominent superheroes The Tick and Arthur.

The Tick: Good morning, America!

Arthur: Hi!

Q: Many questions about you remain unanswered.

T: Hmmm. I am a man of mystery.

Q: Yes, yes. But can you tell me, what do you do?

T: Eh?

Q: I mean, what are your superhuman powers? Can you see through steel?

T: Um...

Q: You know, with X rays? Can you bend iron bars with your mind?

T: Well, I... uh... no.

Q: Can you create energy-based multiples of yourself?

T: Whoa! Nope.

Q: Can you make diamonds out of coal?

T: No.

Q: Shoot heat beams out of your eyes?

T: No.

Q: Breathe atomic fire?

T: No.

Q: Well, then, can you destroy the Earth?

T: Egad! I hope not! That's where I keep all my stuff!

Q: Yes, of course it is. Tell me, do you have a girlfriend?

T: I am mighty! I have a glow you cannot see. I have a heart as big as the moon! As warm as bathwater! We are superheroes, men, we don't have time to be charming! The boots of evil were made for walkin'! We're watching the big picture, friend! We know the score! We are a public service, not glamour boys!

A: Yeah!

T: Not captains of industry. Not makers of things. Keep your vulgar moneys! We are a justice sandwich. No toppings necessary. Living rooms of America, do you catch my drift? Do you dig?

A: I can fly...

Q: And how long have you been a superhero?

T: I guess I've always been a superhero. I don't know much else! I am now, and always have been, simply, The Tick!

Q: How did you enter your career of superheroing?

T: Enter it? I did not enter it. It entered me! It ransacked my heart with its tugs and pulls, threw iron filings of my being into perfect shivering unison, and they all pointed their trembling snouts to the magnetic north of justice! Ya don't get a pension in the hard knocks clambake jungle of superhero life! [clears throat] Where is the juice? I thought there would be juice. Or some kind of pastry, maybe?

Q: How did Arthur become your sidekick?

T: Destiny, that finely shaped engine of the universe with the warm hands and the tasteful footwear, pushed Arthur, wings and all, into my path. We were meant to be together, friends to the end. He has a three-pound brain and it's all smarts!

Q: Arthur, what's The Tick really like?

A: The Tick? He's great! He's a little hard to work with sometimes, but... he's stronger than anybody!

T: Listen! Ours is an epic tale. True friendship! Heart-stopping danger! Men and women in tights! Makin' the rules, and breakin' them! We are not two men. We are ten men!

MEET THE TICK!

JOURNEY INTO THE NATIONAL SUPER INSTITUTE CONVENTION!!!

Superheroes.

You've all seen them, and quite possibly your city may have one or two costumed protectors. But have you ever wondered how and why your local superhero wound up in your town?

Every year, the National Super Institute holds its national convention to decide which new superheroes get the privilege of fighting crime around America. This year's convention took place last week in fabulous Reno, Nevada, and we'll take you there with the young super-hopeful, The Blowfish Avenger. Our story starts a mile off the interstate, off exit 15...

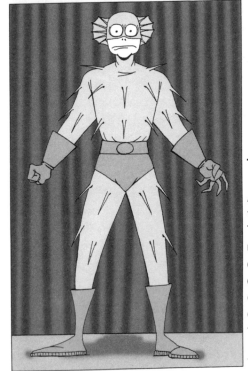

Above: The Blowfish Avenger in "pre-bloat"
Below: Reno's Motel "O"

THE CALM BEFORE THE STORM...

We meet up with The Blowfish Avenger just outside the Reno Motel "O"'s function hall and "Captain Sanity Group Therapy Center." He meets us wearing his unique yellow and green costume. "The costume is a pretty important part of the competition," he says, as he adjusts one of the fins on the side of his head. "As you can see, I put a lot of work into my costume alone!"

And just what can you do as The Blowfish Avenger, we ask? "I'd like to save that for the competition," he says with an intriguing smile, "but I think my powers will prove pretty impressive!"

"The Institute's convention is pretty important," he tells us, "probably the most important event for a young crime fighter, just trying to get started."

We find our way to where the new competing heroes meet. The convention boasts an impressive showcase of would-be heroes this year. Although these heroes are competing against each other, the sense of comradery can be felt throughout the room. In one corner we see the Portuguese Man-O-War helping Jelly Boy on with his jellyfish helmet, and Bi-Polar Bear gingerly shaking hands with The Torso Porcupine. Also, an impressive group of youngsters, wanting to follow in their parents' footsteps, are competing. Jet Valkyrie can be seen with her son, the new Jet Viking, adjusting his jetpack like a proud fussing mother would. The son of longtime hero The Fiery Flame is here. Gifted with similar powers of combustion, he calls himself Friendly Fire.

"I toyed with the name The Fiery Flame, Jr.," he tells us, "but I really wanted

4

MIGHTY BLUE JUSTICE!

to strike out on my own. Get it? Strike out? Like a match? Ha ha!" We hope your crime fighting skills are better than your jokes, Fire. But having your famous father as one of this year's panel of judges surely won't hurt, either.

"There's a great bunch of guys and gals here this year," Blowfish tells us as he looks around the room. "I took some crime fighting seminars with a few of these guys, and let me tell you, they're all pretty good."

Does this affect your thoughts on your chances at the competition? "No, not really. I mean, I think I can put on a pretty worthy display. I think I'm good enough to warrant an assignment in one of the bigger cities, like New York or Chicago, or even The City!"

The City, it turns out, is the Holy Grail of cities for superheroes. "Look who's there already: Die Fledermaus, Sewer Urchin, Crusading Chameleon, The Civic Minded Five... and I don't even have to tell you about the great accomplishments of American Maid!"

Not to mention the super villains who have been known to congregate in The City, too. "Of course villains are important! We all need someone to fight. I heard once, about Fish Boy, the Misplaced Prince of Atlantis, well, he was assigned Bangor, Maine. And he didn't even *see* a super villain for eighteen months. Super villains tend not to make it up to New England too often."

ZERO HOUR!

The convention and competition

starts, and the young hopefuls look on, with wide eyes, nervous smiles, and butterflies in their stomachs. Yet Blowfish seems like he's on top of the world.

The lights go down and the music swells as the night's host, Barry Barrymore, leads his band, The Eventones, and then steps into the spotlight. "I'd like to welcome all you beautiful superheroes! I know you're all excited! We have twenty-six cities to assign to you young heroes...."

The judges are introduced: an esteemed panel of great heroic power and knowledge, Rubber Justice, Earth Quaker, and The Fiery Flame. "Today, the crime fighters of yesterday measure the merits of tomorrow's budding heroes!"

"Now, let's give a big hand to our first hero hopeful," Barrymore announces as The Torso Porcupine takes the stage. Porcupine proudly lifts his arms, as hundreds of deadly spines *sproing* out from his torso and suddenly fire out into a shocked

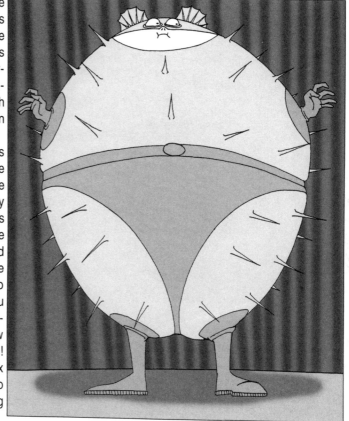

Above: The Blowfish Avenger shows his powers

crowd. The judges look impressed and talk briefly amongst themselves. Seconds later, Torso's future is announced: "Torso Porcupine wins Detroit!" Barrymore proclaims, "Congratulations, Porcupine!"

"Wow. Detroit," Blowfish tells us, "that's pretty good."

And soon it's The Blowfish Avenger's turn up on stage. "Wish me luck," he says to us, as he turns and heads up onto the stage.

In an amazing display,

MEET THE TICK!

RUBBER JUSTICE

The popular and much beloved superhero Rubber Justice may have been given his most difficult mission. Teamed up with Earth Quaker and The Fiery Flame, he faces a tough task: judging the competitors at this year's National Super Institute's Supehero Competition.

Rubber Justice took a few minutes out of his hectic schedule to talk to us.

EPW: *Rubber Justice, why is this competition important?*

RJ: Well, I don't think I have to tell you how important superheroes are in the public's day to day life. Heinous super villains bent on world domination, rampaging giant robots, and hideous mutant monsters are a daily growing threat to the public. The police and national guard can only do so much against such a menace. It takes individuals with super powers, who can fly, burst into flames, control the minds of mortal men, or even stretch, like me, to put a stop to the super-menace. So this competition makes sure that a region gets at least one superhero to deal with the common problems of mad scientists, alien armies, or revenge-seeking plants. Not to mention stopping petty thugs and rescuing kittens out of trees. It's all in a day's work, and it's what the public expects, and deserves.

EPW: *What do you expect to see in this competition?*

RJ: I think we're going to see a fantastic collection of young heroes this year. There's a talented generation out there, just ready to leap from rooftop to rooftop keeping our country safe. I'm sure some of the new faces we see this year will become household names in no time.

EPW: *Any advice to the young hopefuls?*

RJ: A comfortable costume is the key. A costume may strike fear into the hearts of the weak, but if it itches... well, what's the point?

Blowfish suddenly expands his body, puffing out like, well, a blowfish. The crowd gasps with awe and delight. Seconds must seem like hours to our bloated hopeful, as he awaits his assignment.

"The Blowfish Avenger gets New Rochelle!"

The crowd applauds as our bloated hero waddles off stage. "Way to go, Blowfish!"

THE BIG BLUE SURPRISE

The National Super Institute's conventions are always known for their big surprises (who could forget the classic incident between American Maid and Die Fledermaus from a few years back?), and this year is no exception.

Just as The Blowfish Avenger exits the stage, the doors at the back of the hall swing open. A giant blue figure enters, pushing what looks like a large metal box. He lumbers up on stage, to the surprise of both the judges and the audience.

"Hello, Reno! I am The Tick!" he announces as he activates the metal cabinet he's brought on stage with him.

The ominous box opens up, transforming into an automated torture chamber. Knives and blades, drills and spikes, all devices of physical punishment activate themselves. "I am mighty!" boasts The Tick.

"Now you may ask, 'How does one prove one's mightiness?' To this I reply, by surviving the deadliest engine of destruction 1974 had to offer!"

As The Tick climbs into the apparatus he warns us, "You may want to shield yourselves with your dessert menus. I might

be dangerous!"

"This can't be for real," Blowfish says. "I wouldn't worry about this."

But The Tick pulls the lever on his device, and his beastly machine rumbles into activity, resulting in... not much, really. A small hammer strikes this so-called Tick on the forehead.

"I told you. Just another show-off," Blowfish tells us, as a relieved crowd breathes a sigh of relief.

At every convention there is a moment that nobody ever forgets. This is the moment, as The Tick's engine of destruction lives up to its name.

A massive explosion rips through the hall. As the smoke clears and the dust settles, we all see that The Tick, who took the explosion at ground zero, sits completely unscathed! The judges pull themselves together and reward this unorthodox blue champion with his assignment: The City!

"I guess that was a pretty good display of might," a stunned Blowfish Avenger admits.

TO NEW ROCHELLE... AND BEYOND!

And so, after the convention, The Blowfish Avenger heads toward a bus bound for New York. He's had all the proper forms processed and has his permits tucked safely away. He's ready to take on all that New Rochelle has to offer.

"I'm pretty excited," he says. "I think that I can do a lot of good for New Rochelle. I hope that we can all work together, and make my being their civic hero a positive experience."

And what does The Blowfish

MIGHTY BLUE JUSTICE!

Avenger think of The Tick? Did his striking and sudden appearance take any steam out of Blowfish's appearance at the convention? "I don't think so. People like [The Tick] are a real fringe in the superhero community. I don't think we'll be hearing about him any time in the future."

With his luggage safely stowed, The Blowfish Avenger finds a seat on the bus and waves good-bye. "I've got a good feeling about my future... even though, technically, New Rochelle is close to New England."

Below: The Tick with his "Steel Box"

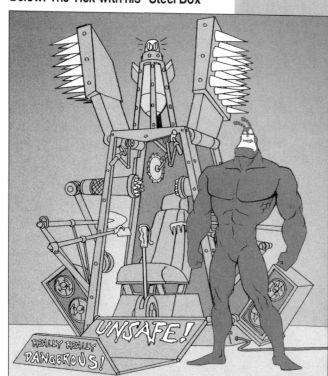

As we all know by now, the big surprise of the National Super Institute's yearly convention was the stunning appearance of The Tick, a superhero so desperate to show us he's got what it takes, he blew himself up... and lived to tell us about it. *Exciting People Weekly* got the scoop, and the first exclusive interview with this exciting newcomer!

EPW: Tick, what brought you here to the National Super Institute's convention?
Tick: I'm proud to say that I traveled here on a bus. Yes, America's road transit is a wonderful way to travel. Some buses even have air conditioning!

EPW: No, I mean what made you come here?
Tick: Oh, I get it. A psyche question! Let me tell you, destiny brought me here. Yes, destiny is a funny kick in the tights: I am destined to be a superhero. And that's no simple path. It's a winding, boulder-strewn path lined with a thousand easy deaths... and no dental plan. My cares are many, and my pleasures are few. Still, this superhero life calls to me. Calls me to Reno.

EPW: You see the National Super Institute's convention as something that is important, then?
Tick: Goodness, yes! All the best new superheroes have

come to this place to compete for the best city in the country to protect. And the piece of the cake with the pretty yummy pink flower on the icing is The City, which I was deservedly assigned to protect from the ravages of evil and super villainy! I mean, anybody could protect, say, New Rochelle. That's pretty lame. But The City! Let me tell you, Ted, The City requires only the most shiny penny as its chosen protector.

EPW: Your Cabinet of Terror; that was a pretty unorthodox way to show your invulnerability...
Tick: No, Ted, I'm not merely invulnerable, I'm nigh-invulnerable. I think I more than proved that, my little inquisitive friend.

EPW: Nigh-invulnerable. I see. But what was the idea behind the performance you gave?
Tick: Let me tell you, last night I was thinking: How can I best express my superhero-ness? As I came here across an ocean of adversity, and after a really long bus ride, with my cheeks ruddy with passion and a heart as big as the moon, the answer came to me: superhuman punishment! A terrible engine of destruction! A big harmful thing! And I think the results speak for themselves.

EPW: It's amazing no one was seriously hurt.
Tick: That's the superhero for you. I never had any doubts.

EPW: Do you think that as a new superhero, you'll be effective in putting an end to crime in The City?
Tick: I don't want to stop crime. I just want to fight it!

EPW: You seem pretty happy with your assigned city.
Tick: Happy? Happy is only a five-letter word for how I feel! Yes, destiny's powerful hand has made the bed of my future, and it's up to me to lie in it! Out there my city lies: unprotected, unloved, crying out for a champion to call its own. A champion to call The Tick!

Official National Super Institute Voucher

Official Assignment:

THE CITY

(Note: not valid with any other offer.)

CITY, IT IS I, THE TICK, YOUR DESTINED DEFENDER... SHOW ME WHERE IT HURTS!

THE CITY... MY THE CITY!

OFFICIAL NATIONAL SUPER INSTITUTE
SCORECARD

Judge: Earth Quaker	Competitor: The Tick
Powers: Nigh-invulnerability	

Comments:

WOW-

Score: 10/10

MIGHTY BLUE JUSTICE!

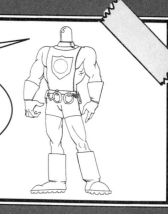

"I HAD MY *SECRET ORIGIN* AT THE NATIONAL SUPER INSTITUTE'S 14TH ANNUAL CONVENTION & COMPETITION! RENO, NEVADA."

MIDNIGHT BOMBER SEZ: "AN OBJECT AT REST CANNOT BE STOPPED!"

FRIENDLY FIRE

For fire and heat-related missions, fire control and manipulation.

"Fighting ice- and cold-wielding villains a specialty!"

YOU'RE NOT GOING CRAZY, YOU'RE GOING SANE IN A CRAZY WORLD!

THE BLOWFISH AVENGER

Proud protector of ~~The City~~ New Rochelle
Call 555-3412 to activate the Blowfish Signal Light!

JET VALKYRIE
Fast! Reliable! Berserk!

NATIONAL SUPER INSTITUTE

14TH ANNUAL
CONVENTION & COMPETITION
RENO, NEVADA

Welcome to the National Super Institute's 14th annual convention in Reno, Nevada. Last year's convention was an exciting success, and we plan to make this year's even better. Among the highlights will be a salute to The Civic Minded Five and a welcome for our guest of honor, Four-Legged Man. Remember, "Let's make a difference!"

We are also pleased to announce that our judges this year are Rubber Justice, Earth Quaker, and The Fiery Flame.

Please take a moment to note the times and locations of events, and remember to fill out your meal ticket if you need a kosher meal.

Friday, the 14th. 2:00p.m. - 5:00p.m.
Hallway
Superhero registration and badge pickup

Friday, the 14th. 2:30p.m. - 2:40p.m.
Main Lobby Hotel "O"

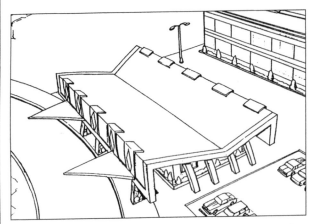

Reno, Nevada's Motel "O," the location of this year's convention & competition

MIGHTY BLUE JUSTICE!

Welcome Luncheon
    Join us for free sandwiches, yummy snacks, and punch, provided by The Comet Club.

Friday, the 14th. 7:00p.m.
Function Hall and "Captain Sanity Group Therapy Center"
Keynote Address
    The National Super Institute officially gets this year's convention started, and welcomes our guest of honor and keynote speaker, Four-Legged Man.

Friday, the 14th. 7:45p.m. - 11:30p.m.
Function Hall and "Captain Sanity Group Therapy Center"
National Super Institute's Annual Dinner Dance
    Join us for what surely will be another memorable event. Jacket & tie or superhero costume required. (NOTE: Please make sure you have a valid meal voucher or no meal can be served.)

Friday, the 14th. 9:00p.m. - 12:00a.m.
The Hoboken Room
Civic Minded Five Slide Show
    A retrospective history of The Civic Minded Five brought to you through the exciting world of slides. Afterward, Four-Legged Man joins us for questions and answers!

Saturday, the 15th. Midnight - ???
The Hoboken Room
Lost In Space Marathon
    Danger, danger! Watch every episode of this classic series on a big screen TV!

Saturday, the 15th. 7:00a.m. - 9:30a.m.
Stiffy's Pancake House
Super Breakfast
    Start your day right, with a trip to Stiffy's famous pancake bar! Orange juice provided courtesy of the Reno Chapter of the Die Fledermaus Fan Club.

Saturday, the 15th. 11:00a.m. - Noon
The Hoboken Room
The Exciting World of Time-Share Condos!
    Your host James "Jimmy" Jim Jones guides you through the world of time-share condominiums in this thrilling and informative slide show. Don't miss it!

Saturday, the 15th. 1:00p.m. - 5:30p.m.
Function Hall and "Captain Sanity Group Therapy Center"
National Super Institute's 14th Annual Superhero Competition
    The event we're all here for, with your host, Barry Barrymore! Twenty-six cities are up for grabs this year. Punch will be provided, and music by The Eventones. (NOTE: Contestants, please meet in the lobby at least 20 minutes before the competition starts.)

Sunday, the 16th. 9:00a.m. - ???
Motel "O" Parking Lot
3rd Annual Mini-Golf Morning
    Catch the bus to Gordon's Goofy-Golf for 18 big holes of mini-golf with Four-Legged Man and other famous crime fighters! (NOTE: Other famous crime fighters to be announced.)

This year's judges: (right) **Rubber Justice**, (below) **Earth Quaker** and **The Fiery Flame**

MEET THE TICK! 11

HOW TO BE A SUPERHERO:
MY 7-STEP PROGRAM TO SUPER-NESS!
BY *THE TICK*

So you think that you want to be a superhero? That's great! The world can't have enough superheroes. But are you sure that you're ready to be a superhero? It's not the life for everyone, and you need to find out if you're cut from the same superhero fabric as... well, me, for instance. Danger lies around every corner and hides under every bed! I've always known that I had to be a superhero. I always was, and always will be, The Tick! And Arthur always knew he needed to be a sidekick (still, he dabbled in accounting; having "options" in your life is fine). But maybe you're better suited to being a dentist. Dentists are also good people! Here are some tips and suggestions that can answer some of your questions and set you down the super heroic path! Oh, and what a path it is, too!

1. Do you have any super powers? If you do, then that's one big important plus. My power of nigh-invulnerability helps me out every single day! Four-Legged Man has four legs! That's a pretty nifty power. Mighty Agrippa is super strong and can fly. Fish Boy just looks full-on weird; a good super power on its own! See, there are lots of different super powers that you can have. Think hard and try to see if you have one. Can you bend things with your mind? Do you have X-ray vision? Can you run really fast? Can you turn invisible? Or maybe you can command the rodent world or talk to dogs. Figure out what you can do that is super heroic, and then try and figure out how you can adapt that to save lives and stop crimes.

2. Do you have neat equipment? Maybe you don't have super powers; not many people do. But after all that doesn't mean you can't be a superhero. There are lots of superheroes who don't have any powers. Look at Arthur! He has no so-called super powers, but he has a nifty suit that makes him fly. American Maid uses her shoes as weapons. Sewer Urchin has a spiky suit and air tanks to

MIGHTY BLUE JUSTICE!

MAKING A SUPERHERO CATCH PHRASE:

"I AM THE ① ② ③ OF ④ !!!"

①

CHOOSE ONE:
MIGHTY, STRONG, QUICK, THRILLING, AWESOME, STUNNING, WEIRD, READY, TRUE-TO-LIFE, RAGING, BEAUTIFUL, INCREDIBLE, AMAZING, HEROIC, FANTASTIC, FAULTLESS, IMMACULATE, UNBEATEN, READY-TO-WEAR, MADE-TO-ORDER, CONSUMMATE, ZINGY, POTENT, EXCITING, VIGOROUS, CAPABLE, ENERGIZED, GLOWING, RAMPAGING, UNPARALLELED, BUBBLY, GALVANIZED, FIGHTING, MAGNETICIZED, FOOTLOOSE-AND-FANCY-FREE, ABLE, SUPER, OMNIPOTENT, FORCIBLE, SWEET, ENERGETIC, DYNAMIC, SPRINGY, ROYAL, EXQUISITE, SINEWY, FORTIFIED, WORTHY, HARDENED, STEELY, ROBUST, INVINCIBLE, SAVAGE, UNCONQUERABLE, SUPERNATURAL, ADMIRED, OVERPOWERING, SHOCKING, OVERWHELMING, ASSERTIVE, BRAWNY, STALWART, STRAPPING, MYSTERIOUS

②

CHOOSE AN ITEM THAT BEST DESCRIBES YOU OR THE PRE-DOMINANT COLOR OF YOUR COSTUME (LIKE FOR ME, IT IS "BLUE!"):
ARMORED, CAPED, DARK, LIGHT, BRIGHT, FURRY, SCALY, SWEET, SLIP-PERY, ITCHY, MASKED, GLOVED, WET, TALL, SHORT, TINY, LOUD, BIONIC, MECHANICAL, ROBOTIC, VITAMIN-FORTIFIED

③

CHOOSE ONE:
HERO, MONSTER, AVENGER, DEFENDER, FIGHTER, ROLLER COASTER, CATTLEDRIVE, CRUSADER, PHENOMENON, POWER DRILL, WONDER, UVULA, NEEDLE, SPECTACLE, COMRADE, TORNADO, BATTLESHIP, CHAMPION, ENEMY, MOUNTAIN, DESTROYER, TREASURE, OPPONENT, ICICLE, LIGHTNING BOLT, CONQUEROR, SURGEON, SUSPENSION BRIDGE, BELIEVER, HAT PIN, DRAG RACER, COMBATANT, BOOSTER ROCKET, SWASHBUCKLER, COMPETITOR, UMPIRE, MASTER, VICTOR, ADVOCATE, FRIEND, SLEDGEHAMMER, SUPERNOVA, PRIZEWINNER, FOE, WELL-WISHER, CONFIDANT, CONSORT, COLLEAGUE, ALLY

④

CHOOSE ONE (POSITIVE):
GOOD, JUSTICE, MIGHT, EXCELLENCE, VIRTUE, NICENESS, VENGEANCE, LOVE, FAIR PLAY, LAWFULNESS, HONOR, GOODNESS, RIGHT, LIBERTY, TRUTH, GOOD-INTENT
OR (NEGATIVE):
EVIL, VILLAINY, SCUM, NAUGHTINESS, WRONG, ILL WIND, OPPRESSION, FOULNESS, INJUSTICE, PESTILENCE, BAD, MALEVOLENCE, HORROR

Example: If I, The Tick, were to use this guide, I might pick **"I am the THRILLING SWEET DEFENDER of FAIR PLAY!"** or **"I am the SHOCKING BLUE DESTROYER of ILL WIND!"**

WARNING: Be careful with this list! It could be used for the forces of evil. If it fell into the wrong hands, we might hear phrases like **"I am the UNBEATEN FURRY MONSTER of INJUSTICE!"** and we wouldn't want anyone to utter those foul words, would we?

Addition on Superhero Phrase by Arthur

I don't think that a superhero's catch phrase needs to be as organized as what The Tick recommends. I mean, I think that you can get by with whatever comes naturally to you. I like to say, "Not in the face! Not in the face!" And by saying it twice, that really gives it the "oomph" that makes it special. Well, that's what works for me, anyway.

15

MEET THE TICK!

SIDEKICKS

Sidekicks are fine citizens, and an important part of the superhero way of life. They are cute little junior superheroes that fight along side you, and a little behind you. They help you out, and if you're really lucky, your sidekick can become your best friend!

You might decide that your best means of entering the superhero society is as a sidekick. Learning under the example of an experienced crime fighter is a wise thing to do. It's the choice that Arthur made, and just see how great that has worked out!

Or maybe you are a full-fledged superhero who wants a sidekick. Maybe you are lonely out on patrol, but the "super-team" lifestyle isn't for you. Sidekicks are the answer! They're useful, because they often come up with good plans for escape, or help out in fights by taking on those pesky little henchmen, leaving you free to go after the main baddy. Also, villains LOVE to kidnap sidekicks, which can be an excellent start to an all-new adventure.

No matter which side of the sidekick coin you want to be on, you have to agree that sidekicks are a swell part of the super life!

MIGHTY BLUE JUSTICE!

GOOD SIDEKICK VS. BAD SIDEKICK

ARTHUR:

BETTER-THAN-AVERAGE ACCOUNTANT'S BRAIN, WITH THREE BIG POUNDS OF SMARTS. I'M UTILIZING ARTHUR'S BRAIN ALL THE TIME!

FLYING SUIT. GIVES ARTHUR ALL THE DEXTERITY AND FLYING ABILITY OF A MOTH (WHICH COMPARED TO THAT OF AN EAGLE IS NOT TOO GOOD, BUT IS STILL BETTER THAN A FLYING SQUIRREL'S. NOW THAT WOULD BE REALLY LAME). PLUS, THE SUIT ISN'T TOO "FLASHY." REMEMBER, IT'S NOT FAIR TO YOU OR YOUR SIDEKICK IF HIS SUIT IS COOLER THAN YOURS. BUT ARTHUR HAS A SKILL (FLYING) THAT I DON'T HAVE, SO WE CAN HELP EACH OTHER OUT, ALTHOUGH ARTHUR HAS TROUBLE CARRYING ME WHEN HE FLIES. HE CAN ONLY FLY DOWN WHEN HE CARRIES ME. BUT WE'RE WORKING ON IT!

ARTHUR CURVES IN ALL THE RIGHT PLACES. *ONE BIG CURVE!*

INTERVIEW WITH ARTHUR

The media just desires to know everything they can about my exciting exploits. Many citizens enjoy a phenomenon called "Talk Radio" in which people "talk" about "issues" and broadcast them through America's exciting radio broadcast system. One such show wanted gripping insight into my daring exploits, but they broadcast their show during the hours of the terribly important early-morning patrol, so I couldn't attend. In my place, the always-ready-to-talk Arthur became the guest on the show.

Later on, I discovered that I could send $29.95 to the radio station, and they would provide me with a transcript of the show. So here it is, for those of you who may have missed hearing it on your very own radio!

Roger: It's now 8:32, and we'll have traffic at the top of the hour. Welcome back to the City Morning Zoo, right here on WCTY, and we have a special guest here in the studio.

Rick: We sure do, Rog.

Roger: That's right, Rick. Remember running around your backyard with a towel tied around your neck pretending to be a superhero?

Rick: You bet I do, Rog.

Roger: It was probably last week, wasn't it?

Rick: How'd you know? Oh, you crack me up!

Roger: Well, we all wanted to be a superhero at one time or another. But most of us grew out of that.

Rick: Most of us discovered girls!

Roger: Something you'll never have.

Rick: Ouch! You sting me!

Roger: Just kidding, my friend. But seriously, some people don't give up on being a super-hero, and we wanted to talk to one such individual.

Rick: Yep, but we couldn't get one.

Roger: Yeah, I wanted to talk to that American Maid. Ooh!

Rick: She could clean my dishes!

Roger: It'll never happen, my friend.

Rick: Oh! Again with the zingers!

Roger: Yep, American Maid declined our offer to be on the show this morning. Something about "dignity."

Rick: Blah, blah, blah.

Roger: So we managed to find someone without dignity. Just kidding. We have a very special guest— Arthur.

Arthur: Uh, hello everyone.

Roger: You're not really a superhero, though, are you?

Arthur: Well, I guess I'm more of a sidekick. But being a sidekick is pretty important.

Roger: I'm sure it is. That's a nice little suit you have on. What are you, some sort of Bunnyman?

Arthur: No, I'm a moth.

Roger: A moth? Don't moths have wings?

Rick: Moths have wings.

Roger: It's decided! Moths have wings. I don't see any wings. You're a bunny!

[laughter]

Arthur: No! I do have wings. They retract.

Roger: Oh, they retract.

Rick: Retractable wings. Clever.

Roger: Yeah, like your retractable brain, Rick!

Rick: Ouch! You got me there!

Roger: I kid. It's a fun show. You having fun, Arthur?

Arthur: Sure, I guess. I've never been on the radio before.

Roger: Really? We couldn't tell.

[snickers]

Roger: So... you became a moth. So what happened? You were a scientist and got bitten by a radioactive moth in a top-secret experiment gone horribly wrong?

Arthur: No. I was an accountant. One day I came across the moth suit. And I figured that was the way for me.

Roger: You turned your back on accounting?

Rick: Hard to believe!

Arthur: Accounting is a fine skill to fall back on, but the road less traveled... much less traveled... the moth and wings road, it's a lot more exciting than taxes.

Roger: You're sidekick to, uh... The Tick, right?

Arthur: That's right.

Roger: How'd you and the big blue guy get together?

Arthur: The Tick calls it destiny. I was walk-

MIGHTY BLUE JUSTICE!

ing home one day, after, uh... leaving my accounting job, and he fell off a building right in front of me. Ever since then, we've been fighting crime, and he's been sleeping on my couch.

Roger: On your couch? No Tick cave?

Arthur: None that I know of.

Roger: Stunning. Stunning story, there. So with your wings...

Rick: Retractable wings!

Roger: Retractable wings, that's right. So with the retractable wings, how fast can you fly?

Arthur: Well, I don't actually fly much. It's more like gliding. I can fly a little bit, but I'd rather not.

Roger: So you couldn't, say, fly around the Earth really fast and turn back time?

Arthur: No. Besides, I don't think time would reverse if the Earth rotated in the other direction. I think the sun would just rise in the west.

Rick: I think time would go backwards.

Roger: Me, too. Let's take some calls! Caller, you're on the air. Do you think time would go backwards if the Earth turned the other way?

Caller 1: Uh... yeah, I guess...

Roger: Thanks! Next caller! Hi, you're on!

Caller 2: Hi. I have a question for Arthur.

Roger: Ask away.

Caller 2: What's it like being The Tick's sidekick?

Arthur: It's great! The Tick is probably my best friend. He was there to really help me get my own crime fighting career started. He gave me my first big push.

Rick: Ha! Right off a building, I bet!

Arthur: Actually, that's right. He did push me off a building. That's how I learned to fly.

Rick: Oh. I was just kidding... about the roof... thing...

Roger: It looks like you're just not funny, Ricko! Say, Arthur, do you have any advice for any of the listeners out there, who, themselves, might want to become a superhero sidekick?

Arthur: Being a sidekick is something you really have to want to do. Like I said, I felt a need to answer the call of adventure! But I guess the most important thing that I can tell anyone is to just be, well... careful.

Roger: And you need a costume. Where did you get your moth outfit, Arthur?

Arthur: At a garage sale. It took me some time to get the nerve to try it out, though.

Roger: Garage sale? Well, there's a helpful tip for our listeners.

Rick: You never know what you'll find at a garage sale.

Roger: True. That's where we found you, Rick! Ha ha! Let's go to our next caller. Hello? Question for Arthur?

Caller 3: This is for Arthur. Yeah. Do you have any tax advice?

Arthur: Be honest, pay on time, and keep good records of your receipts.

Caller 3: Thanks!

Roger: We have time for one more. You're on with Roger, Rick, and Arthur!

Caller 4: Arthur! You're on the radio!

Arthur: Tick?

Caller 4: That's right, chum. I was monitoring the local radio for crime. The radio can be a very fine resource for information.

Roger: Hey! Good to talk to you, Tick!

Caller 4: Yes it is! I have a question for your guest.

Roger: Go ahead...

Caller 4: I... uh... can't remember that... thing... you told me last night...

Arthur: Tick! It's easy! You enter in the time, then you press the power button on the microwave.

Caller 4: Aha! Now, yummy hot popcorn shall be mine! I've been listening to you, Arthur! You're doing great! You've got quite a lovely speaking voice. Good going, chum!

Roger: Wow. Popcorn. Well, Arthur, we're out of time. But I think we've learned a lot.

Rick: I know I have.

Roger: Rick, you haven't even learned to dress yourself in the morning.

Rick: Oh, the comedy!

Roger: So thanks for being here this morning, Arthur. Our guest was Arthur. He's a superhero side kick, and his new book is... don't you have a book out, Arthur?

Arthur: No, I don't.

Roger: Oh. Well... thanks for being on the show, anyway.

Arthur: Thanks for having me.

Roger: Coming up next, traffic and weather, then after the news it's Dr. Kelly Kellerman, telling us about her whipped cream diet!

Rick: Fab!

MEET THE TICK!

19

Color coordinating your tights and loading up a utility belt is just the beginning to a fantastic superhero career. Today's successful superhero needs a secret headquarters and a villain-busting crime lab. A place to hold your amazing super arsenal and all your equipment, like supercomputers with blinking lights and informa-tion screens and paper printing out all over the floor! Somewhere to keep your collection of persona-oriented vehicles and "mobiles," like your car, plane, boat, helicopter, motorcycle, jeep, tank, hang glider, submersible, zeppelin, rocket ship, and pogo-plane!

The best place for a secret hideout is a cave under-neath your mansion. Caves usu-ally allow you easy access to roads and rivers, and have great big openings that you can fly your jets and things in or out of. Plus caves are keen because they're real hard to find! Another really good place for your base is Antarctica. Just about nobody lives there, so rent is cheap, and you can build giant fortresses right out in the open, and still, no one will know! But Antarctica is really far away and really really cold, not only in the winter, but in the summer, too!

It's possible a few of you don't have easy access to caves and Antarctica. But all is not lost. There are some alterna-tives. Believe it or not, some superheroes have managed to turn their very own apartments into their secret headquarters. The best part is that you can switch back and forth between a regular swingin' bachelor pad and a super-swell crime-busting lab! So when your perimeter warning detector goes off and alerts you that kindly Aunt Martha is coming down the hall to bring you a new batch of

MY SECRET HEADQUARTERS! (ARTHUR'S APARTMENT)

MIGHTY BLUE JUSTICE!

nice warm cookies, you can hit your secret activation-transform-mo-switch, and turn your head-quarters BACK into an apart-ment, and act like nothing is going on. Woo hoo! Aren't you just atingle thinking about it?

Here's how you can turn your apartment into swell superhero digs (some of these plans may call for tools such as power saws, screwdrivers, and advanced computer equipment):

— Things that "flip" around are good. Get as much flipping and retracting action into your room as possible.
— Coffee table can flip around into the floor and become a real-ly swell radar screen, with maps and arrows and weather information, and the screen should be circular, with a line like a clock hand that spins around real fast on the screen. It should make a sound like *boop!* and enemies should show up as a blinking red dot on the screen.
— Your couch should flip back into the wall and become this entire computer-crime-lab setup. There

should be little computer and television screens and all kinds of buttons and switches and blinking lights! Blinking lights are great! From here you could also communicate with police headquarters and other super-heroes working out of their own secret bases. Your computers have got to be easy to use. If you've ever used a home com-puter, you'll know that they're really complicated, so you have to get a computer setup that does exactly what you want by just pressing one really brightly colored button. The buttons should also light up when you press them. Those kind of but-tons are the best! There should also be somewhere where you

can get all sorts of neat comput-er printouts. They should come out on big long rolls of paper that just keep pumping out! Or maybe on those secret-looking cards with holes punched in them.
— One whole wall should slide back to reveal a giant video screen. The best wall would be the wall behind your couch (see last tip) so that your command console can directly interface with your giant view screen. From this screen you could talk to other heroes, and look right at them! There would be a little built-in camera that looks at you, so the other superheroes could see you, too! Two-way video conferencing! You can also

MEET THE TICK!

see crimes in progress and get information and maps and all sorts of stuff, telling you where evil is taking place. See evil as it happens! Get some satellite hookups, too. Orbiting satellites are a valuable source of information. There could also be lots of other little television sets, giving you live satellite updates from far-off places like London, Madrid, and Mars!

— A bookcase can turn around to reveal all your crime fighting equipment. Here you can have all sorts of boomerangs and shields and grappling hooks and rope and a special high-powered gun to launch the ropes to a building across the city. There could also be a crime-lab setup here, for all your sneaky detective work. You need beakers and test tubes and twisty glass tubes moving multicolored chemicals around. Heat them up with a Bunsen burner! A smaller computer would be installed here that could instantly analyze fingerprints and samples of clothing and dirt.

— It's important to have a table, somewhere, where you can have meetings and conferences with your sidekick, or maybe other visiting superheroes. It's always cool to have your superhero logo painted right on the tabletop! Your dining room table could flip over into the floor to produce your special meeting table. You could turn your whole dining room into your command center!

— Pictures and clocks and framed things can all slide back and reveal television screens, pumping-in vital information. I can't stress how important TV screens are. After all, we are living in the Information Age!

— Your normal refrigerator full of normal snacks can turn into a super-refrigerator full of super-snacks! My favorite super-snacks are those little boxes of juice that come with the little bendy straw. Neat!

— Your closet should open up to reveal the place where you keep your costume (when you're not wearing it). If you can get some sort of mannequin to wear it, it looks really impressive, especially when you have spotlights that are automatically activated to shine on your costume when you approach it. You might also

22

MIGHTY BLUE JUSTICE!

have "variant" costumes that you could keep here, too, like your aqua-deep-sea-diving costume, your arctic costume, your special mechano-battle armor, a zero-gee space-suit or radar reflecting stealth suit.

— A skylight is a great thing to have. It gives you instant access to the roofs of the city, where you conduct your daily and nightly patrols. And a skylight looks really stylish! Or a grandfather clock could slide away to reveal a pole or a slide to whisk you to your crime fighting vehicle of choice.

— Lots of satellite dishes and rotating radar emitters are great things to have on your roof. The problem is, they kind of draw attention to themselves (and you!). However, I don't know how to conceal them. Maybe you could throw a blanket over them.

— Most importantly, you need some sort of lever that will activate your entire headquarters system. Something stunningly normal-looking, like a coat hook or a candlestick or a book that when you move it, it activates all your stuff! Causes it to open up, and turn around, and buzz and blink with activity. It's so exciting!

The problem that you may run into is that there always seems to be somebody there saying, "You can't tear up the floor," and "The landlord will get angry," and "We can't afford that!" (Afford? Can you afford not to?) To which all I can say is, "Arthur! 'Can't' can't be in your vocabulary when it comes to proper anticrime hardware!" Still, sometimes we must compromise. So here are some things you can do to affordably help out in your fight against villainy.

— A television is a good start. Televisions tend to provide you important news at both six o'clock and eleven o'clock.

— A really good magnifying glass. You can look at all sorts of stuff!

— Use a pair of binoculars to monitor space (at night).

— Computers are useful. I'm not sure how to use one; they're super-complicated. I saw this one computer where you could actually shoot at little alien spaceships. Cool! Get one of those!

— You can't go wrong with a telephone. You can call just about anyone. And they can call you, too!

— A digital clock. They can even tell you the time at night. Arthur's has an alarm that activates on its own to tell us when patrol time is.

— You could probably still put super-snacks in a regular refrigerator.

MEET THE TICK!

23

PLANS FOR A "TICK-MOBILE"

-MAP LIGHT. GOOD.

-STEERING WHEEL. GOOD.

-DASHBOARD COMPASS. GOOD.

THESE ITEMS ARE ALL GOOD. WE CAN KEEP THEM. THE REST MUST GO!

PROJECT 16-D: THE TICK-MOBILE

THE PLAN: TO TURN ARTHUR'S SISTER'S CAR FROM THIS TO *THIS*

— Super jet engine. Shoots lots of flames out the back and looks really cool. Will make the car go really, really fast.

— Big Tick battering ram on the front of the car. Good for knocking things down.

— Fins!

— 2 Bubble canopies, for me and Arthur. We can keep the map light and compass here. And an onboard supercomputer that can operate the car all by itself! And it can talk, and it will call us by name. It will say, "Hello, Tick," when I get in the car. It will also know when some unauthorized evildoer is trying to steal the car. It will grab them with a big steel belt and hold them while warning alert sirens go off and confetti shoots into the air.

— Drink holders!

— 2 big Tick antennae, that can pick up radio and television signals, and a direct computer linkup (if we had a computer to link up to...).

— A big claw arm that comes out of the front of the car that can pick up villains and carry them away!

— Shiny blue nigh-invulnerable paint.

— 2 really big thick tires on the back.

— Air bags and really good seat belts. Safety first!

— A super-spoiler-wing thing.

— A big flashing blue light that says, "Out of the way! Justice coming through!"

— A swiveling cannon that can shoot smoke bombs and ropes and pretty fireworks.

— Really bright headlights.

TOP SECRET!

NOTE: SOME CARS I'VE SEEN ON TV CAN TURN INTO GREAT BIG ROBOTS! LOOK INTO HOW THAT IS DONE.

Tick,
We can't afford to make this car. Besides, I don't think Dot would let us.
- Arthur

MIGHTY BLUE JUSTICE!

THE TICK'S GUIDE TO BOMB DEFUSION

1. FIND BOMB.

2. DECIDE WHAT KIND OF BOMB IT IS.

THIS KIND OF BOMB OR THIS KIND OF BOMB

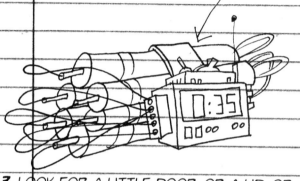

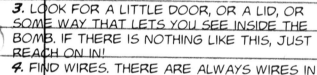

3. LOOK FOR A LITTLE DOOR, OR A LID, OR SOME WAY THAT LETS YOU SEE INSIDE THE BOMB. IF THERE IS NOTHING LIKE THIS, JUST REACH ON IN!

4. FIND WIRES. THERE ARE ALWAYS WIRES IN BOMBS. MOST OF THE TIME, THE WIRES ARE ALL SORTS OF PRETTY COLORS. USUALLY THE WIRES GO BETWEEN A CLOCK THINGY AND THE ACTUAL EXPLOSIVE STUFF. SOMETIMES EXPLOSIVE STUFF IS EITHER STICKS OF DYNAMITE, OR SOME LUMPY PLASTICENE STUFF.

5. PULL SOME WIRES OUT. BOMBS NEED WIRES TO WORK. IF THEY DIDN'T, THEY WOULDN'T HAVE WIRES. WITHOUT WIRES, BOMBS DON'T BLOW UP. (NOTE: IF THE WIRES ARE ALL SORTS OF COLORS, AVOID THE RED WIRE. LEAVE IT ALONE. RED IS BAD. DO NOT PULL OUT THE RED WIRE. TRY THE BLUE ONE.)

6. THE BOMB IS NOW DEFUSED.

3. I DON'T KNOW HOW TO STOP THESE KINDS OF BOMBS FROM BLOWING UP.

4. TELL EVERYONE AROUND YOU TO RUN AWAY, THEN HOLD BOMB OUT AT ARM'S LENGTH, AND LET IT EXPLODE (WORKS BEST IF YOU ARE NIGH-INVULNERABLE, LIKE ME!).

MEET THE TICK!

Sally Vacuum: That was the scene today, at the Rive Droite Bank, as the mysterious gang known as "The Idea Men" struck again, continuing their terrible crime wave. It was the sixth time in as many days that the baffling criminals have descended from the sky to literally "lift" The City's most valued assets. But today, their nefarious plot was thwarted by a heroic blue stranger:

The Tick: Hey cool! They got a blimp!

Sally Vacuum: Our modest blue benefactor exited the scene without comment. But The Idea Men menace is far from over, says Mayor Blank:

Mayor Blank: ...in fact, we have reason to believe that these criminals have merely been "practicing" for a much larger caper.

Sally Vacuum: We'll have more on this story as it develops.

IDEA MEN THREATEN TO DESTROY HYDRO-ELECTRIC PLANT!
EVIL PLOT STOPPED BY THE TICK!

THE CITY - The Idea Men showed up again last night, this time at The City's hydroelectric plant. While the Idea Men were difficult to understand, they got their threats across: deliver a ransom of ten million dollars, or the dam would be blown up, flooding the city.

When asked if he would give in to these terrorists' demands, Mayor Blank replied, "Let me put it this way... how well can you swim? Ha ha, but seriously, we have no choice. They have our dam, and no force on Earth can stop them now."

Although the ransom money was handed over to The Idea Men, payed out of municipal tax funds put aside for such villainous threats, The Idea Men activated their bomb anyway.

Fortunately, The City's new sworn protector, The Tick, was on hand. "No time to talk, I've got a bomb to defuse," The Tick told us as he ran into the dam. When we asked a small man in a white bunny suit, who accompanied The Tick, if he had bomb defusion experience, he told us, "I don't know. It never really came up in conversation. But he must, or he wouldn't be trying... right?"

Rather than defusing the bomb, the clever blue avenger used The Idea Men's own bomb to destroy The Idea Men's blimp. Idea Men floated down safely into the hands of waiting authorities.

The Tick commented on the future safety of The City: "Our future holds still more dire threats... more perilous plots! Wherever villainy rears its great big head, wherever evil sets its giant, ill-smelling foot, you will find The Tick!"

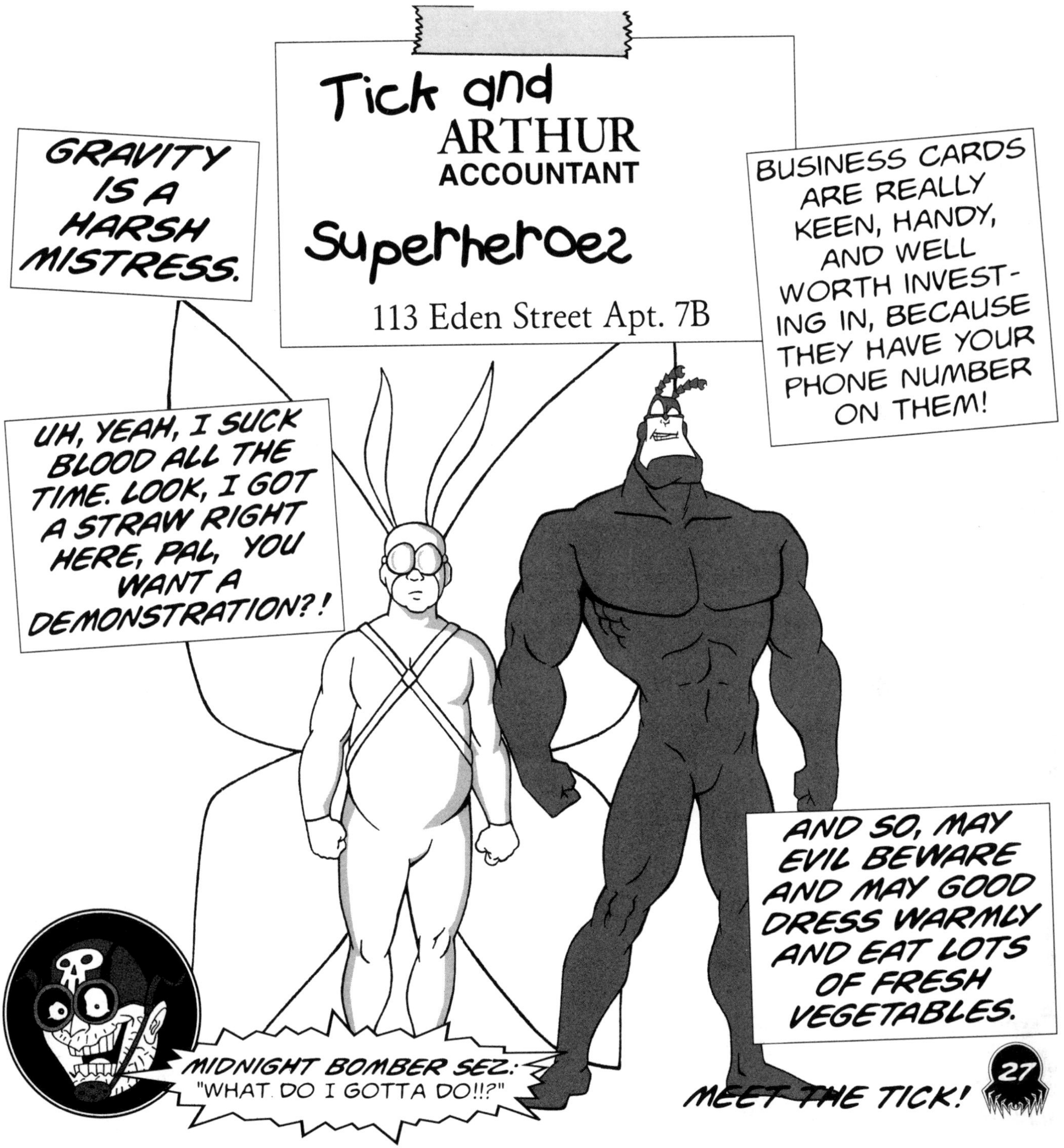
Tick and ARTHUR ACCOUNTANT Superheroes
113 Eden Street Apt. 7B
GRAVITY IS A HARSH MISTRESS.
BUSINESS CARDS ARE REALLY KEEN, HANDY, AND WELL WORTH INVESTING IN, BECAUSE THEY HAVE YOUR PHONE NUMBER ON THEM!
UH, YEAH, I SUCK BLOOD ALL THE TIME. LOOK, I GOT A STRAW RIGHT HERE, PAL, YOU WANT A DEMONSTRATION?!
AND SO, MAY EVIL BEWARE AND MAY GOOD DRESS WARMLY AND EAT LOTS OF FRESH VEGETABLES.
MIDNIGHT BOMBER SEZ: "WHAT DO I GOTTA DO!!?"

PART 2: THE TICK'S GUIDE TO SUPERHEROES

    While, yes, it is true that I am a thorn in the side of evil, it would make sense that many thorns in the many sides of evil would really put a cramp in evil's bitter day. And that is why there are other superheroes. I know that I alone could handle the never-ending fight against villainy, but why would I want to? Teaming up with other superheroes is keen!

    Here are some notes that I've made for my Secret-Tick-Database about the other heroes that I know and have shared adventures with.

American Maid

    She is said to be the world's most patriotic domestic, and she really is! American Maid and I (and Arthur. Don't forget Arthur!) have worked together defeating many a foe.

Superhero-ness: I don't think she has any true super powers, but she's kind of pretty (not that I have time to think about "that sort of thing" — the pursuit of justice is a jealous girlfriend that doesn't want you noticing the legs of another woman). American Maid has amazing gymnastic skills. She's a red, white, and blue rubber ball, bouncing in the name of good. She has impressive hand-to-hand fighting skills. I've seen her knock many a villain absolutely loopy! American Maid's shoes were made for fightin'! By merely kicking her shoes off her feet, I've seen her disarm a gun-toting fool at 50 feet, and pin a grown goon to a wall.

Notes: She is kind of bossy.

28

MIGHTY BLUE JUSTICE!

Die Fledermaus

Die Fledermaus is The City's dark avenger of the ~~night. Which must be when he does all his crime-fighting,~~ because I usually see him sitting in Ben's Diner all day, drinking those big expensive coffees with all that foam ~~and mysterious brown powder sprinkled on top. EEE-~~ YUCK! And $3.95 for a coffee? Not for me, friends: A cold ~~glass of lemonade will never steer you wrong.~~

Superhero-ness: Die Fledermaus has a nifty utility belt ~~on which he carries all sorts of things. The utility belt~~ holds many secrets! But so far all I've seen in the belt are ~~bandages and Band-Aids and quarters for pay phones.~~ Still, I can't criticize. A superhero must be prepared!

Notes: Something is going on between Die Fledermaus and ~~American Maid. These two don't send each other warm~~ fuzzies, but cold pricklies. Take note of this when organiz-ing team-ups and group outings.

Sewer Urchin

Sewer Urchin is the pungent avenger of the ~~underworld (the underworld of the sewers, that is— I~~ don't think he has any horrid supernatural connec-~~tions). Urchin must be doing a good job, because I~~ rarely hear of any sewage-related misdeeds.

~~**Superhero-ness:** There's no nice way to put this:~~ Sewer Urchin just stinks! But this is a great example of making good use of your established talents in the fight against evil. For those villains with the mighty strength to make it past Sewer Urchin's powerful ~~odor, he's smartly adorned himself with many sharp~~ spikes. A fine weapon, yet rough on the furniture.

Notes: Possibly not the best candidate for long road ~~trips.~~

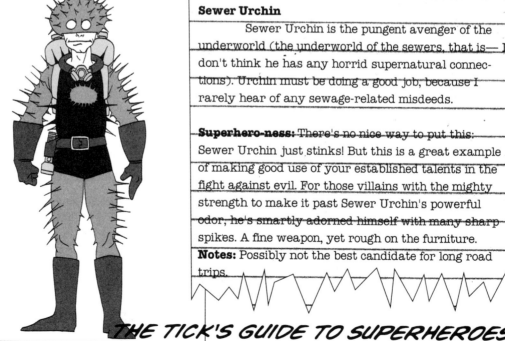

THE TICK'S GUIDE TO SUPERHEROES

The Human Bullet

Many superheroes can fly. Many can't. Although The Human Bullet cannot fly, he doesn't let this hold him back! That's the attitude! Knock your limitations square on the chin.

Superhero-ness: The Human Bullet is himself, in a way, a weapon. When the need arrives, he loads himself into his giant cannon, and with the help of Fire Me Boy, he launches himself into the evil eye of crime. He may not be accurate all of the time, or even ANY of the time, but for someone so dedicated as to perform such a feat, who are we to judge inaccuracy?

Crusading Chameleon

Color changing to help in the fight for right! Is there anything you can't do in this great country?

Superhero-ness: Crusading Chameleon has a mighty spiffy costume, which he uses in this war on evil. The costume has the ability to change to match the color of anything he is near. Red, blue, yellow, orange, green, and even puce and a tasteful beige. His sticky little fingers and toes allow him to creep along the walls and ceiling, too. So as you can see, the name "Crusading Chameleon" isn't just a clever moniker!

Notes: Don't let him get near anything... complicated.

MIGHTY BLUE JUSTICE!

Big Shot

Big Shot used to be one big, walking train wreck of a superhero. He wanted to hold evil in check at gun-point, ~~when in fact he was holding his inner child at gun-point~~, and this turned him into a one-man-army-of-crazy! I've said it before, and I'll say it again: guns and super-heroes don't mix! ~~Fortunately, Big Shot has, in fact, done~~ the best thing he could to keep the world safe. He sought the help only a good psychiatrist and angora can offer.

Superhero-ness: Not much of that going on here, my friend. Except the fact he could run around with that big ~~trunk of weaponry on his back. What a balancing act!~~
Notes: Big Shot's advice: "Keep anger in the Happy Box." The Happy Box, indeed.

The Civic Minded Five

The Civic Minded Five are The City's mighty group of protectors. Once, the five fought individually, but realized as a team they could get a joint bank ~~account and tax breaks on a clubhouse. Wise choice.~~

The current members of the Civic Minded Five are: Four-Legged Man, Jungle Janet, The Carpeted Man, Feral Boy, and Captain Mucilage.

Four-Legged Man

Four-Legged Man is the leader of The Civic Minded Five, and does, in fact, have four legs, all working together in the fight for justice! And ~~Four-Legged Man can often be heard saying, and this is something I take~~ to heart, "With four legs comes great responsibility!" Yes, Four-Legged Man, it does.

Superhero-ness: Four legs! Wow! Four-Legged Man uses this awesome power to catch twice as much evil as a two-legged hero does.
Notes: ~~Four-Legged Man is the leader of The Civic Minded Five, and thus~~ must perform all the traditional roles that a superhero team leader must, such as taking roll call and shouting their motto, "Let's make a difference!" Swell motto!

Jungle Janet

Jungle Janet is another member of The Civic Minded Five. Man, is she one mighty woman! Seven feet tall with arms like tree trunks, yet with a soft, feminine side.

Superhero-ness: Amazing amazon strength! Jungle Janet sports a snazzy little leopard-spotted number for her superheroine outfit. Nice!

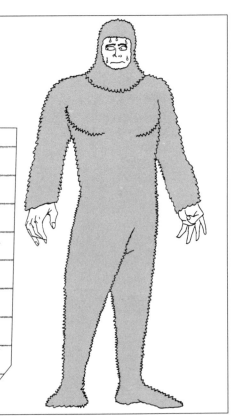

The Carpeted Man

The Carpeted Man: amazing master of static electricity. I think we've all had a run-in with static electricity, and know the stinging pain!

Superhero-ness: The Carpeted Man has made an ingenious suit of carpet, with which he can build up a static electrical charge by walking over any surface. Any surface! And think—we walk over surfaces every day!

Notes: This fellow sure sweats a lot.

MIGHTY BLUE JUSTICE!

Feral Boy

Feral Boy is the bare-chested avenger, and requisite Civic Minded Five member who can barely control his savage side. That aside, he's a good Feral Boy. Good boy, indeed.

Superhero-ness: He works that animal angle, and he works it well. He fights like an ape, and is hungry like the wolf. He drools up a load, too.

Notes: Of all the superheroes I know, I like playing "fetch" with Feral Boy the most.

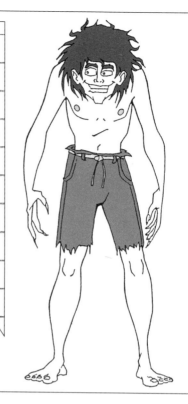

Captain Mucilage

When crime gets sticky, the answer is glue! And glue is the weapon that Captain Mucilage uses in the war on crime. What more can be said?

Superhero-ness: Captain Mucilage wears a suit with a mighty, built-in glue deployment system that shoots high-powered mucilage at his enemies.

Notes: Remember not to shake hands with Captain Mucilage. Greet him with a polite "hello," and then avoid the handshake by pretending something has caught your attention and distracted you. Avoid the handshake at all costs!

THE TICK'S GUIDE TO SUPERHEROES

Don't see that much of him these days...

Mighty Agrippa, Roman God of the Aqueduct

This guy is a class act all the way! He talks like a superhero, walks like a superhero, even eats like a superhero. I mean, no crumbs, no slurping, and no sauce or juices on his chest. He even has real-life super powers!

Superhero-ness: Mighty Agrippa can do all sorts of things! He can fly, has superhuman strength, and has the mighty power to transport any volume of water from one location to another. How can evil even face themselves in the morning, when they know that this kind of power opposes them?

Notes: Mighty Agrippa will let you try on his keen hat, if you ask real nice.

Fish Boy is our moist avenger, who keeps the waterways safe for truth, justice, and frolicking on the beach!

Superhero-ness: Fish Boy must have super powers. He's got these big fishy eyes, and he's green. And that sort of thing just ain't regular!

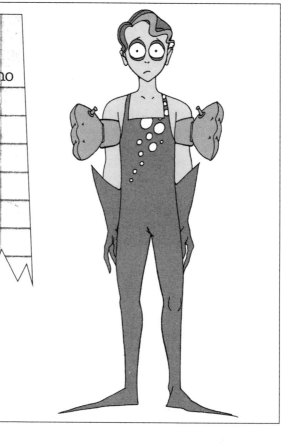

Jet Valkyrie

Jet Valkyrie is the stainless steel provider of justice. She's one fast and shiny woman, that's for sure.

Milkie, the Milk Boy

I don't know what he does, but I met him at Stuart's Food Castle, and he had a keen costume, and he gave me a wholesome good glass of milk, so he's okay in my book (that's this book, in fact)!

Doorman

Doorman works at the fabulous Comet Club and has the urgent responsibility of protecting the door. It's his duty to only let true superheroes in, and keep the riffraff out! And the sidekicks, too. In a class-less society, he wouldn't have this duty, but have you looked at some people's sidekicks? Man, they just have no class! And their eating habits! EECH!!! But I don't have that problem—Arthur is one class act!

Superhero-ness: Doorman can fly and has the uncan-ny strength of a biker guy twice his size. He also has his "Doorman-sense" that alerts him of tragedy, such as a sidekick sneaking into the Comet Club.

MIGHTY BLUE JUSTICE!

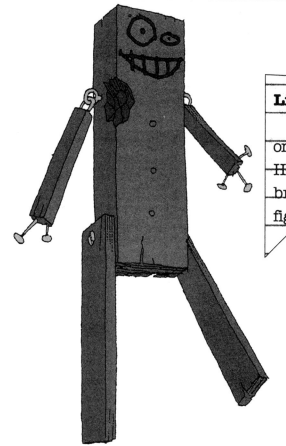

Little Wooden Boy

Little Wooden Boy was my sidekick once. I... I don't really want to talk about it. ~~He gave his life... to... to save ME! What a brave little soldier! It was a great honor to fight the forces of evil with him.~~

Plunger Man

Plunger Man is one of the newest and bravest new heroes to hit the scene in a really, really long time. He gives me faith in the future.

Superhero-ness: Plunger Man carries a super toolbox that contains his stunning arsenal, with such amazing do-good weapons as... a plunger! He also knows how to put your arms back on your body if they ever fall off (which could happen—you never know). His uncanny instincts seem to put him right in the action when he is needed.

THE TICK'S GUIDE TO SUPERHEROES

Carmelita

Carmelita is just like Arthur. Well, actually, she's not like Arthur at all. She just dresses like him. She also usually smells nicer than Arthur, too.

Superhero-ness: Carmelita dons the mighty moth suit and can fly around and do all the mothy things with it. She is also quite brave and smart but still... she likes to kiss! Some people need to learn that there's a time and a place for everything, and kissing has no time or place in a super heroic career.

Notes: Carmelita's very own father, J.J. Eureka Vatos, invented the flying moth suit that both she and Arthur wear. What a neat dad!

FEEL THE NEED TO LEARN?
THEN FLIP TO PAGE 76!

MIGHTY BLUE JUSTICE!

Eclaire

Eclaire is Belgium's greatest superheroine. She has all the coolest super powers, and she uses them in the fight for truth, justice, and the Belgiumese way of life!

Superhero-ness: Eclaire has a bunch of really keen powers. She is super strong, can fly, and, best of all, can shoot lightning from her eyes. Wow! Talk about "Euro-power!"

Notes: ~~Eclaire is French for "lightning!"~~ And, I think, French for a yummy pastry dessert.

Blitzen

Blitzen is the superheroine sidekick of Eclaire. She, too, keeps Begium safe and free, and does all the other stuff that Eclaire does. And she drives around on a real boss motor scooter, too!

Superhero-ness: She calls herself "righteous speed-demon and trust fund darling of justice." And who am I to argue?

Notes: Blitzen is german for "lightning!" Man, just how many languages do these Belgians speak? How do they say "lightning" in ~~Belgiumese~~?

THE TICK'S GUIDE TO SUPERHEROES

INTERESTING PEOPLE I HAVE KNOWN

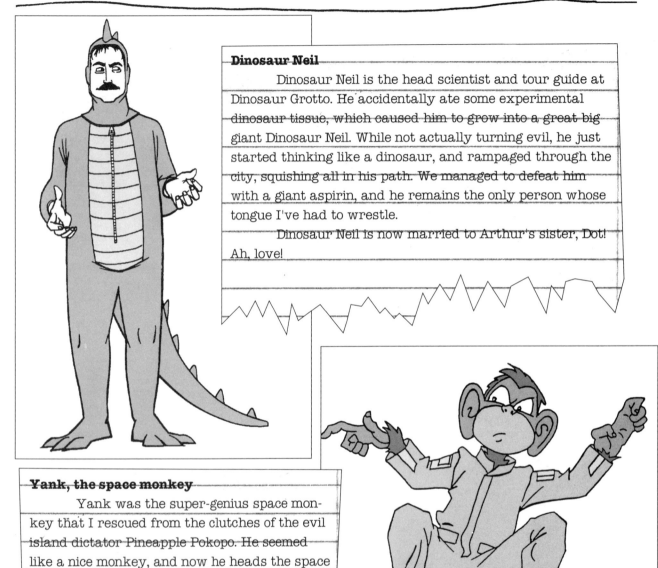

Dinosaur Neil

Dinosaur Neil is the head scientist and tour guide at Dinosaur Grotto. He accidentally ate some experimental dinosaur tissue, which caused him to grow into a great big giant Dinosaur Neil. While not actually turning evil, he just started thinking like a dinosaur, and rampaged through the city, squishing all in his path. We managed to defeat him with a giant aspirin, and he remains the only person whose tongue I've had to wrestle.

Dinosaur Neil is now married to Arthur's sister, Dot! Ah, love!

Yank, the space monkey

Yank was the super-genius space monkey that I rescued from the clutches of the evil island dictator Pineapple Pokopo. He seemed like a nice monkey, and now he heads the space program. And who says America isn't the land of opportunity?

MIGHTY BLUE JUSTICE!

The Mole-Men

The Mole-Men are my keen little friends who came to visit from the Subterranean World. They are the Mole-King, King of the Mole-People; Bob, Minister of Mole Defense; Todd, Minister of the Exterior; and Larry, Minister of the Treasury. They're really neat little guys, but don't try to feed them snails!

Blow-Hole

Man, this cat just has to run. But he's no cat, oh no! He's a giant whale-guy who runs and swims around the world again and again and again. Nobody knows why, but I like to think he does it for the love of it! Arthur and I were once stuck in Blow-Hole's tummy. If it wasn't for the bravery of my one-time sidekick, Little Wooden Boy, we'd be there till this day still.

Leonardo Da Vinci

What a keen guy! He can invent all sorts of things, and they really work, too!

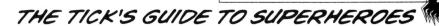

THE TICK'S GUIDE TO SUPERHEROES

Captain Sanity

  Captain Sanity was my psychotherapist and head psychiatrist at Captain Sanity's Superhero Sanatorium. He was a pretty good doctor for a severed head being kept alive in a jar.

Taft

  Taft is cool! And boy, can he wear a mustache! However, I didn't really like it when Captain Sanity would have Taft dress up in costumes and beat me up as "physical therapy."

The Whats

  The Whats are neat little space-alien dudes that came to get me to save the universe! It's keen how they thought of me to save everybody! Look! They've got three eyes!

MIGHTY BLUE JUSTICE!

Captain Decency and the Decency Squad

Captain Decency and the Decency Squad are spectacular super-heroes from yesteryear. They all had exciting adventures fighting crime and villainy back in the days when everything seemed to be black and white. They faced off against such classic villains as The Terror, The Sub-Human, and Joseph Stalin! Now, when I have time, Arthur and I go and visit the Decency Squad, now living in Commander Good-bye's Superhero Retirement Home, and listen to their inspirational tales of old-fashioned crime busting and the glory of our superhero heritage.

The Decency Squad included:

Captain Decency— With his sidekick, Johnny Polite, he led the Decency Squad through many amazing adventures!

The Visual Eye— He could fire his eyes out and see at long distances when he yelled "Rockets from the sockets!"

The Living Doll— He's full of tinier men!

Sufrajet— She flew at amazing jet speeds right into our hearts!

ONLY 33 PAGES LEFT TO 76, THE EDUCATIONAL CHAPTER!

THE TICK'S GUIDE TO SUPERHEROES

The Ladies of SHAVE

The Agents of Project SHAVE were three groovy chicks who traveled around with dorky Special Agent Jim Rave, hunting a rogue mustache. They were:

Kitty Zangatu - Ninjitsu, demolitions, electrolysis!

Holly Golovely - Kung fu, demolitions, she-devil with a comb!

Crystal - Liberal arts, demolitions, red-hot with a hair dryer!

Corduroy Cordoba

Corduroy Cordoba is the night watchman at Aztec City, and a man of mystery! He gave me the straight skinny on those jerky Aztec kids.

MIDNIGHT BOMBER SEZ: "YEAH! KEEP PLAYING WITH FIRE, SUPER-PANTS! YOU DON'T KNOW HOW MUCH FIRE YOU'RE PLAYIN' WITH!!"

MIGHTY BLUE JUSTICE!

44

Julius Pendecker

Julius Pendecker is the genius inventor of Pendecker Laboratories. He's always coming up with new devices, robots, and superweapons. Why? Because he can. But between you and me, I can't understand a word that little guy says.

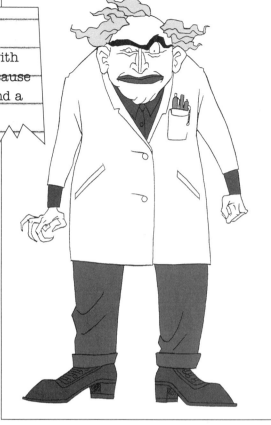

King of Belgium

He was the nicest King of Belgium I've ever met.

MIDNIGHT BOMBER SEZ: "BAD IS GOOD, BABY!! DOWN WITH THE GOVERNMENT!!"

THE TICK'S GUIDE TO SUPERHEROES

Back | Forward | Home | Reload | Images | Open | Print | Find | Stop

Go To: http://www.americanmaid.com/

The Unofficial American Maid Home Page

Welcome to the Unofficial Home Page for the country's greatest superhero, the world's most patriotic domestic, <u>American Maid</u>. <u>American Maid</u> is a <u>brilliant strategist</u>, dedicated fighter, and courageous hero who's not afraid of <u>commitment</u>. Here you will find all the latest information on American Maid's most <u>recent adventures</u> and <u>enemies</u>, plus <u>background information</u> about American Maid, her <u>superhero skills</u> and her <u>weapons</u>. Also visit the <u>American Maid Chat Room</u> and talk about American Maid with many of her other admirers around the web. Updated 4/28. This page looks best with Microscape 2.0.4.7.3.1beta-gold. <u>Click here to download Microscape now!</u>

American Maid news:

<u>American Maid</u> recently completed a successful mission against <u>Pineapple Pokopo</u>, the evil dictator of <u>Pokoponesia</u>, an island nation whose most abundant resources are <u>pineapples</u> and <u>sharks</u>. The mission was to rescue the famous <u>American</u> space monkey <u>Yank</u>. <u>American Maid</u> was aided on the mission by other notable <u>superheroes</u> <u>The Tick</u> and <u>Arthur</u>.

- Click here to go to the <u>Pokoponesia Tourism Web Page</u>.
- Click here to go to the <u>National Space Program Page</u>.

Here's what's available on the American Maid Home Page:

- <u>Vital statistics</u> about American Maid.
- American Maid's <u>mission information</u>.
- American Maid's <u>combat skills</u>.
- American Maid's <u>weapons</u> and <u>shoes</u>.
- American Maid's <u>allies</u> and <u>Die Fledermaus</u>.
- See <u>thumbnails of American Maid gifs</u> to download.
- <u>Download QuickVid clip</u> of American Maid's appearance on *Heroes*.
- <u>Download sound clip</u> of American Maid: "You guys take the direct route. I'll come down through the roof. And don't let them retreat. It won't take Chairface long to figure out you're just a diversion."(34k)

Other cool American Maid related links around the Internet:

- <u>Julie's American Maid Home Page</u>.
- <u>Donna's Other American Maid Home Page</u>.
- <u>Sarah's Other Unofficial American Maid Home Page</u>.
- <u>The Die Fledermaus Sucks Web Page</u>.
- <u>The Official "I Hate Die Fledermaus" Page</u>.
- <u>Die Fledermaus Is a Dork</u>.
- <u>Doom</u>.
- <u>The Official Dinosaur Grotto Page</u>.
- Albert's *Heroes* <u>Episode Guide</u>.
- <u>Official Annual Flower Show Home Page</u>.

There have been **6755** visitors to this page :)

Click here to <u>e-mail</u> American Maid

This page is created and maintained by **Prudence.** Visit **Prudence's Home Page!**

MIGHTY BLUE JUSTICE!

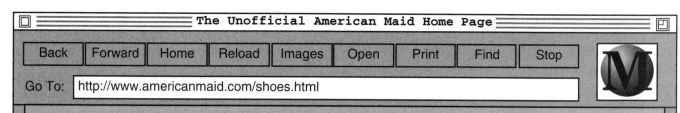

| Back | Forward | Home | Reload | Images | Open | Print | Find | Stop |

Go To: http://www.americanmaid.com/shoes.html

American Maid's Shoes

<u>American Maid</u> uses her high <u>stiletto shoes</u> as powerful <u>thrown weapons</u>. She is a master of the <u>projectile high-heel shoe</u> and can pin a <u>fly</u> to the wall at fifty paces. She can kick her shoes off her feet with equal accuracy. In the rare chance that she misses an intended target, the shoes are designed to complete a <u>boomerang</u> arc and fly back to her.

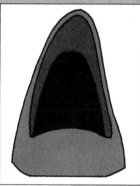

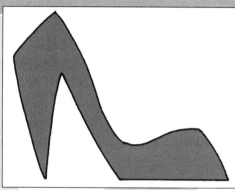

● <u>Click here</u> for a list of suggestions on how to turn your <u>shoes</u> into deadly weapons. List was originally posted in <u>alt.americanmaid.shoes.weapons</u>.

● Click here to visit <u>Shoe-Net</u>.

<u>Back to The Unofficial American Maid Home Page</u>

Click here to **<u>e-mail</u> American Maid's shoes.**

This page is created and maintained by **<u>Prudence</u>**. Visit **<u>Prudence's Home Page!</u>**

Die Fledermaus

"A complex hero for a complex world"

MIDNIGHT BOMBER SEZ: "AND SO I GO, I SAYS, 'YEAH BABY! A GIMMICK! THAT'S IT! HIGH EXPLOSIVES!!!'"

DIE FLEDERMAUS GAVE ME THIS WHEN I ASKED HIM IF HE WANTED TO CONTRIBUTE TO THE BOOK.

MIGHTY BLUE JUSTICE!

Die Fledermaus

Name: Die Fledermaus
Real Name: TOP SECRET!
Base of Operations: The City, and for a week each year, Hollywood
Group Affiliation: Loner
Height: 6' 4"
Weight: 225 lbs.
Teeth: White

Super Powers: Unknown! Die Fledermaus is a creature of the night, come to The City from parts unknown. Die Fledermaus is an enigma; is he a startling visitor from a far-off planet, a mysterious supernatural force, or a fearless mortal putting the safety and well-being of others before his own? All that needs to be known is Die Fledermaus is looking out for you! Never again need you fear darkened alleyways, the crime-riddled streets of the East End, or the shady water-front district. An ever-vigilant watchman upon the skyscrapers of The City, Die Fledermaus is a complex hero for a complex world!

Weapons & Equipment: Die Fledermaus relies on a wide assortment of weapons and equipment, the most important being his silk-lined cashmere cape (see enclosed booklet "Die Fledermaus and His Fearsome Cape!"). In times of danger, when The City is held in the grip of villainous evil, Die Fledermaus's justice can be summoned with "The Die Fledermaus Signal." Die Fledermaus's mask contains incredibly sophisticated microcircuit-powered sonar emitters, giving him a Sonar-Sense™, making it impossible for crooks, thieves, and crimelords to escape his icy gaze of justice. Special claws have been specially installed on Die Fledermaus's boots, to aid in Die Fledermaus's special "kick and gouge" fighting style, the mere mention of which leaves villains shaking with fear. They also aid in traction, when running is important. Die Fledermaus uses a special utility belt, containing a virtual arsenal of crime fighting equipment: The Die Fleder-Grappling-Hook™ and Die Fleder-High-Powered-Pressurized-Hook-Launcher™, Die

Die Fledermaus
"A complex hero for a complex world"

To The Tick-Man, Best Wishes, DF

Fleder-Rope™, Die Fleder-Smoke-Bombs™ of all colors and flavors, Die Fleder-Tackers™, Die Fleder-Hypno-Spray™, Die Fleder-Knockout-Gas™, Die Fleder-Two-In-One-Bug-Repellent-And-Sunblock-32™, and other Die Fleder-Equipment™ too numerous to list. Die Fledermaus is always prepared!

Super Villains Die Fledermaus Has Defeated (to date): The Idea Men, Dinosaur Neil, Mr. Mental, El Seed, The Evil Midnight Bomber What Bombs at Midnight, Proto-Clown, The Swiss, Chairface Chippendale, Multiple Santa, Brainchild, The Ottoman, The Deadly Bulb.

Other Lesser Superheroes Whom Die Fledermaus has Helped Out: American Maid, Sewer Urchin, The Tick, Arthur, Fish Boy.

What the media has had to say about Die Fledermaus:

"Masked Superhero Saves the Day!"

"Caped Mystery Man Keeps City Safe at Night"

"Die Fledermaus is... Good... Superhero"

"Die Fledermaus... Help in Stopping Bank Robbery"

"Does The City Need More Superheroes Like Die Fledermaus?"

"...Heroic..."

"...Strong..."

"...A True American Wonder..."

"The City Needs... Die Fledermaus"

"Award Winning Performance"

"One of the Year's Best"

"Two Big Thumbs Up"

"Die Fledermaus Cuts Ribbon at New Tanning Salon"

"Hero of the Month (October)" — *Leotard Legends* magazine

"One of the Year's 100 Best Heroes" — *Crime Fighters Illustrated*

"Our Favorite Guest Walk-On" — *SOD (Soap Opera Digest) This Week*

Die Fledermaus Résumé

Education: Graduated the Gorgazon School of Male Modeling. Graduated from three-week Dayton School of Telemarketing night school course. Graduated top 15% of class.

Achievements: Competed at the 9th Annual National Super Institute Convention. Assigned to The City.

Work Experience: World-class superhero for the last 5 years
Conducted seminar "How to NOT Take It in the Face" at 12th Annual National Super Institute Convention
Celebrity judge in Wiscassett County Fair Pie Competition
In chorus in the Second National Touring Company of *HMS Pinafore*
Two years of male footwear modeling—won "Second Runner-up Male Footwear Model of the Year"
Understudy to "The Stage Manager" in the Woodrow Wilson High School production of *Our Town*
Led the Arbor Day assembly at George Washington Carver Junior High School
Cowrote and played "Fuzzy Bunny #3" in City Public School #14's production of *The Fuzzy Bunnies Welcome Spring*

To contact Die Fledermaus, please feel free to use the Die Fledermaus Signal weekdays, found at City Police Headquarters.
(NOTE: Signal is most visible from dusk to dawn.)

MIGHTY BLUE JUSTICE!

What other nationally known superheroes have to say about Die Fledermaus:

"I know him! I welcome the chance to 'team up'! Besides, he's got a great big cape!" — The Tick

"Die Fledermaus looks very impressive." — Arthur

"Yeah, Die Fledermaus. He's a superhero. Definitely a superhero. Yeah." — Sewer Urchin

"Die Fledermaus is... one of the biggest... superheroes that I've... worked with." — American Maid

Deertown T.V. Listings - **Saturday the 5th**

43

MIGHTY BLUE JUSTICE!

Sanitation Gazette's Man of the Year:

SEWER URCHIN

The streets and skies have long had their own super-heroes, looking out for our safety and well-being. But there has always been one important area of The City that has been overlooked: The City's Sewage System. Overlooked until now! We are happy that we now are blessed with our own crusader, wading through the waste, keeping the tunnels safe and free. A mysterious avenger whom we are proud to name our Man of the Year: Sewer Urchin!

After presenting Sewer Urchin with his award at a modest ceremony held last week at the Sanitation Main Office on Lower Reese Boulevard, we had the privilege to talk with Sewer Urchin.

Sanitation Gazette: Sewer Urchin, this must be a proud day for you, being named Man of the Year?
Sewer Urchin: Yeah. Big day. Very big day. I'm really happy. Happy to be Man of the Year. Yeah. Mom would be very happy.
SG: The crime rate is down in the sewers by a stunning 100%. Do you feel that you can take credit for this amazing statistic?
SU: Yeah. It's definitely because of me. Yeah.
SG: What made you decide to be the "Champion of the Sewage System," as it were?
SU: It sounded like a really easy job. Really easy. And to tell the truth, the crime rate was 0% before I became Sewer Urchin.
SG: That odor. Is it you?
SU: Most of it, yeah.

Most of the odor is me. It's my weapon against crime. Odor fights crime. I work in the sewers. I do some of my best work there.
SG: Besides your amazing out-fit, do you have any other crime fighting equipment you use in your mission to keep the sewers safe?
SU: Yeah. I've got a lovely submarine.
SG: A submarine. How did you acquire a submarine?
SU: I found it in the sewers. You'd be amazed what you'll find down there. I also found a toaster oven, a nice pen set, a big set of encyclope-dias, a very beautiful couch, and a videotape machine. The encyclopedias are missing *L* and *N*, and the VCR is Beta. Can't complain, though. Definitely can't complain.
SG: What's the biggest menace you have faced in the sewers?
SU: Once this big steaming Lava-Man showed up. Yeah, but he just kept running through the sewers. Ran away. Otherwise, I would have had to deal with him. Punch!
(continued on page 16...)

53

BIG SHOT

and that's why the A52-B Rhino-Dropper is my ammo of choice.

ATPJ: But, Big Shot, what weapon do you recommend for the young gun-toting vigilante, just starting out?

BS: Let me tell you, you can't go wrong with the new Sleeman Semiautomatic Self-Cleaning AK-63b. It's light and affordable, but man, oh, man, can it deliver a punch! If this model was out when I was getting started, things would have been much easier for me. Plus, it has the option of fantastic expandability. For a vigilante who wants to invest a little more start-up funds, he can add a 96F NightVision-O-Matic scope and an 876-GAuto-Super-Clip. That's a good package to get you started and out there on the streets. Now for anyone who is really, really serious, I suggest they look into pur-chasing a *(continued on page 44...)*

GUNS AND SUPER-HEROES DON'T MIX. SEEK PROFESSIONAL HELP.

SCIENTIFIC PSYCHOPATH

Why didn't you love me, Mommy?

The tragic story of the so-called superhero Big Shot, and the Super-Psychiatrist that saved him.

"Put anger in the Happy Box." That is the simple mantra that has worked miracles with Big Shot, the gun-toting, "break all the rules" vigilante who used violence to fight crime, and to try to solve all his own problems.

MIGHTY BLUE JUSTICE!

Secret Headquarters's Top 10 Training Rooms.
#7 Crusading Chameleon

MIGHTY BLUE JUSTICE!

PART 3: THE CATALOGUE OF VILLAINY!

All good superheroes should keep extensive records and files on the numerous masters of evil that they encounter. An understanding of what makes their evil little brains bubble and pulse is the first step on the road to defeating them. And what a long and winding road it is!

These records, ideally, should be kept on a giant supercomputer, with a screen as big as your wall! Perhaps by just speaking the villain's name into the computer, it gives you all the dirt you'd need about the evildoer, and then spits it out for you on a nifty little punch card! But Arthur showed me the stark economic reality of a supercomputer versus a notebook, and the notebook won. Still, a notebook has a certain low-tech charm, and so, here it is.

I've made up some important categories to help me classify each and every villain. It makes it easy, and it looks real official, too!

Evil Powers: Most super villains have evil powers that cause them to commit evil. Quite frankly, if they didn't have evil powers, they probably wouldn't be super villains. They'd probably keep their acts of horror restricted to poor tipping in restaurants, and taping music from their friends' CD collections.

Physical Oddness: Yes, just about all villains have a physical oddness that starts them on that wicked, wicked road. How many good, outstanding folks have tentacles?

The Bad Plan: Their little scheme for world domination or unfathomable riches.

The Idea Men

Evil Powers: The Idea Men use the powers of organization to the goals of badness. They all work together, misusing guns and bombs. They even found a way to exploit a blimp for villainy! Egads!

Physical Oddness: They each wear a mask that makes it just plain maddening to understand what the heck they're talking about! Enunciate, for crying out loud!

The Bad Plan: It seems this bunch wanted to steal a lot of money so that they could quit work and spend like the demons they were.

BOMB

MIDNIGHT BOMBER SEZ: "BOOM BOOM!"

Chairface Chippendale

Evil Powers: Chairface has been at this evil racket for quite a while and has amassed an impressive stockpile of evil devices and evil friends. Watch out, 'cause he practices his sword fighting!

Physical Oddness: He's got a chair for a head! Now you know how that sort of thing messes with your melon!

The Bad Plan: The big show-off wanted to write his name over the Moon! What's that all about?

Kids of America, think twice! When you flip that coin of behavior, choose Good! And don't wait 'til it hits the ground—call it in the air! 'Cause if you choose Evil, you could end up like these guys: (back) Hooks Horowitz, Boils Brown, Zipperneck (IK!), The Deadly Nose, Headless Henderson, Harriet Curse, The Butterfly-Nutcase, (front) The Forehead, Eyebrows Mulligan, The Crease, Jack Tuber — Man of a Thousand Faces, Sheila Eel, The Guy With Ears Like Little Raisins, Dyna-Mole.

MIGHTY BLUE JUSTICE!

Professor Chromedome

Evil Powers: Professor Chromedome is one of the many that uses his horrible brain for further horribleness.

Physical Oddness: For protection against falling things, or reasons far beyond any of us to understand, Chromedome has encased the top part of his head (and, naturally, his brain) in a stainless steel dome. He also speaks in an awful (and really fake) German accent.

The Bad Plan: Chromedome works for Chairface Chippendale, and has created his arsenal of rotten. Some of the professor's devices include The Poison County Carpet, Doom-Jelly, The Notorious Dogs-Playing-Poker, and the Moon Menace Heat Ray, which was used in the ultimate act of lunar vandalism.

YOU WILL LEARN SOME REALLY USEFUL INFORMATION IN JUST A FEW PAGES, WHEN YOU REACH PAGE 76!

Mr. Mental

Evil Powers: Besides his semi-impressive mental powers used for long-distance-remote-hypnotism and similar "whatnot," he has strange powers of misconception—for instance, he has disguised his evil schemes as an entertaining stage act.

Physical Oddness: Bald.

The Bad Plan: He once tried to steal the experimental Thinking Cap to enhance his abnormal powers to do all sorts of terrible things.

THE CATALOGUE OF VILLAINY

The Breadmaster

Evil Powers: He bakes in the name of evil! He has the recipe for exploding and expanding bread bombs, muffin grenades, and the deadliest of cakes.

Physical Oddness: He's not too odd, but he has a swingin' mustache, and we all know how dangerous those can be!

The Bad Plan: He once held The City ransom for the ingredients to bake the fearsome City-Smothering Lemon Soufflé! The horror of it... but I do have to say the Breadmaster commits the best SMELLING crimes!

Buttery Pat

Evil Powers: He's the assistant to The Breadmaster, which is an evil act in itself, but Pat also has the bizarre powers of being slippery.

Physical Oddness: It looks to me that he's made out of butter! He oozes and drips, and is just plain weird!

The Bad Plan: Like I said, he helps out The Breadmaster, whose evil plans are bad enough for the two of them!

MIGHTY BLUE JUSTICE!

El Seed

Evil Powers: El Seed is an evil scientist flower, who can create potions that give him control of plants. Evil manipulation of plants? What could be worse, I ask?

Physical Oddness: He's got a flower for a head, which is mighty uncommon, for the citizens whose Zip Code is GOOD. His hands are all leafy-like, making it tough to put the cuffs on this one!

The Bad Plan: He not only used his potions to turn plant against planter in the quest for plant domination, but he made me sprout broccoli from my mighty shoulders!

The Bee Twins

Evil Powers: The Bee Twins do the bidding of El Seed, and use their flying and stinging to aid the evil plant.

Physical Oddness: Their voice! It's full-on weird. They talk at the same time. How do they do that? And they fly. They fly all around. And sting. Oh, how they sting.

The Bad Plan: They are right there to do El Seed's bidding, pollinating the flowers of horror.

THE CATALOGUE OF VILLAINY

Rosebud

Evil Powers: Rosebud is one of El Seed's super-strong, super-thorny, and super-evil plant creations. Rosebud seems to have the strength of an entire field of roses!

Physical Oddness: He's a seven-foot tall, super muscular plant-thing, with a pretty red rose for a head.

The Bad Plan: The poor creature just mindlessly does the bidding of his vile master, El Seed. Is that so wrong? The answer is YES!

Barry

Actually, poor misguided Barry isn't really an evil villain. He's just a superhero gone terribly wrong! He thought that he could walk around calling himself "The Tick," so I had to fight him for the name. And if I fight you, and I am GOOD, then where does that leave you? Right on Santa's "naughty" list, that's where!

Evil Powers: Barry has a shield with a kinetic generator that gives him superhuman crushing power. But Barry's biggest evil power is the power of his attitude.

Physical Oddness: Drool, man! Drool!

The Bad Plan: He thought he would just be a big bully, and be "The Tick." Being a bully is just about the lowest of bad plans, kids. Remember that!

MIGHTY BLUE JUSTICE!

Brainchild

Evil Powers: This tyke is yet another in a long tragic line of evil geniuses. He uses all his super smarts to enter the Science Fair of Villainy.

Physical Oddness: Unlike most kids his age, who want to show off their individuality with a unique haircut or a slanted fashion sense, Brainchild likes to show off his individuality (and his brain) by encasing his upper head in a glass dome. And that kind of odd is just not right!

The Bad Plan: Using his robot dog, Skippy, he built a Mega-Devastator-Multi-Cannon, and used it to actually try to crash the Moon into the Earth. Hasn't the Moon suffered enough?

The Evil Midnight Bomber What Bombs at Midnight

Evil Powers: He likes to blow things up, and let me tell you, a rotten mind and high explosives just don't mix!

Physical Oddness: Just listen to him. This guy's nuts!

The Bad Plan: He wanted to be the biggest of the bad. He figured by blowing up the fabulous Comet Club, the hot spot for superheroes on their night off, he could be known as the villain who got rid of all the heroes The City had to offer.

BOMBS

CAREFU

Thrakkorzog

Evil Powers: Thrakkorzog has an evil brain, bent on conquest of our dimension. He also has quite an assortment of cosmic devices at his disposal, to help him carry out his bidding, including the horrid Clonerizer.

Physical Oddness: Besides being a giant interdimensional oozing slug, his tongue alone has an unholy appetite for destruction—and brains!

The Bad Plan: Thrakkorzog wanted to create an entire army of clones made from ME! Imagine the horror and confusion of an Evil Tick Army! Despite all this, I understand he makes a pretty decent roommate.

Evil Mucus-Tick Clone

Evil Powers: Mucus-Tick possesses all my strength and power, along with the ability to mutate and mush up his body. He can slide down pipes and turn in to an entire blob of mush. But foul Mucus-Tick's worst power is the ability to plain gross you out!

Physical Oddness: While he does bear my handsome likeness, he's green and see-through. Remember, I'm so thick with might, you can't see through me!

The Bad Plan: Mucus-Tick was created to carry out Thrakkorzog's terrible bidding. The only way for me to defeat him was to suck him back into the nasal cavity from which he was born.

MIGHTY BLUE JUSTICE

Pineapple Pokopo

Evil Powers: Pineapple Pokopo is the evil dictator of the island nation of Pokoponesia. Although his fist is normal, he rules with an iron one. He exploits all the resources at his disposal (which is predominantly sharks and pineapples) to enact his evil bidding.

Physical Oddness: His head is rather oddly shaped. That is, if you think a pineapple is oddly shaped.

The Bad Plan: Pineapple Pokopo's dream is to conquer Hawaii, and then move on to Wyoming.

Lava-Man

Evil Powers: Lava-Man is made up of not only fiery molten rock but fiery molten evil. He burns stuff up with just a mere touch. And, boy! Is he ever strong!

Physical Oddness: If being made of lava isn't enough, he's also really, really big. And orange!

The Bad Plan: Lava-Man was sent on a mission to assassinate my little friend, the Mole-King. Fortunately, because the Lava-Men are from the Subterranean World, you don't run into them too often.

THE CATALOGUE OF VILLAINY

Proto-Clown

Evil Powers: Proto-Clown has the strength of a baker's dozen of angry clowns! He's as destructive as a regular clown is funny. Actually, he's even MORE destructive!

Physical Oddness: Unlike most clowns, Proto-Clown is about 20 feet tall and his funny red nose honks for EVIL!

The Bad Plan: Proto-Clown doesn't really have an "evil plan," but he sure does like to smash and bash and crash and just plain bust stuff up.

The Terror

Evil Powers: If pure evil were ever personified, it would have to be The Terror. This guy is just plain bad.

Physical Oddness: The guy is like 115 years old! The dark forces of just plain bad are the thing that keeps this guy going.

The Bad Plan: Over the years, The Terror has had more evil plans than all the other super villains combined! The guy tried to punch out a national monument, for gosh sakes! Even a normal super villain wouldn't take things that far!

MIGHTY BLUE JUSTICE!

Tuun-La

Evil Powers: Tuun-La is a space monster and has all the typical evil powers that space monsters tend to have.

Physical Oddness: I guess for a space monster it doesn't look that odd, but to the human eye, look out! Even if you ignore the pinchers, the orange skin, and the ugly dress, the thing has two mouths! See if that doesn't give you the willies!

The Bad Plan: Like all space monsters, Tuun-La wants to conquer the Earth. And by teaming up with the likes of The Terror, this beast has made a frightening start.

Stalingrad

Evil Powers: Possesses all the dreadful evil powers that the original Stalin had.

Physical Oddness: Looks just like Stalin. That mustache...! NO!

The Bad Plan: Because he possesses all of Stalin's evil powers, it is safe to assume he also wants to carry out all of Stalin's evil plans. Whatever they may have been.

The Man-Eating Cow

Evil Powers: We all think that The Man-Eating Cow lives up to her name. And who wants to be eaten? By a cow, no less?

Physical Oddness: Most cows don't crave human flesh. Also, The Man-Eating Cow looks just like an ordinary cow, so you never know just when or where The Man-Eating Cow will jump out of a herd and get you!

The Bad Plan: This is hard to say. To my knowledge, The Man-Eating Cow hasn't ever been seen eating anyone. But she did get mixed up in the company of The Terror.

THE CATALOGUE OF VILLAINY

Swiss Industrial Spies

Evil Powers: The Swiss Industrial Spies carry these super Swiss Army Knives that can turn into various weapons that poke and gouge and shoot. They also have helicopter blades and telescopes and all sorts of nice things, too. What a pity that such wonderful devices are put to use for evil.

Physical Oddness: They all have funny accents.

The Bad Plan: They wanted Arthur's pants!

Omnipotus

Evil Powers: Omnipotus has amazing cosmic powers. He's not really evil, I guess, but he lives by eating planets, and eating a planet, especially MY planet, has to be considered an evil act!

Physical Oddness: For such a big guy, he's got freaky small feet!

The Bad Plan: I lived with... or rather ON... this guy for two months, and then he tried to eat the entire planet Earth! By my saying that I'd be his friend, he spared the Earth and didn't eat it. But he still did take a bite out of the poor old Moon....

MIGHTY BLUE JUSTICE!

Venus

Evil Powers: Venus has the power to cloud the hearts of men, and uses the power of love, normally a fine power to have, as a power of evil.

Physical Oddness: It's not gentlemanly to point out such things, but between you and me, Venus hasn't missed a meal.

The Bad Plan: She wants to be the baddest of the bad, and that isn't good.

Milo

Evil Powers: He seems to have one of those evil-inventing minds. He created a device that made my arms fall off and built the Evil-Tick-and-Arthur-Robots.

Physical Oddness: Well, you wouldn't catch ME wearing the costume he runs around in.

The Bad Plan: He does all that the evil love goddess Venus commands.

Multiple Santa

Evil Powers: Multiple Santa can create many, many evil Santa clones. This is possibly the most horrendous and evil power any super villain could have. It's wrong for just so many reasons!

Physical Oddness: He looks like Santa, but he sure doesn't act like Santa.

The Bad Plan: The worst possible plan — to destroy Christmas and steal a whole bunch of stuff.

THE CATALOGUE OF VILLAINY

The Mother of Invention

Evil Powers: This little man went and invented a working time machine that he wears on his head. He can also get his vile little hands on bombs (but I don't know if he makes them or just buys them).

Physical Oddness: It's not polite to stare, but he has this ugly little thing on his face.

The Bad Plan: He kidnapped all the great inventors of the past, and then planned to blow up the past and reinvent the inventions in the future. Huh? Does that make any sense? I don't know, but I think this Mother of Invention is just a petty little man.

The Deadly Bulb

Evil Powers: The Deadly Bulb controlled electricity and thus controlled our lights. And nobody, I say nobody, should be without light when they reach for that little chain dangling below the lamp! The Deadly Bulb also has a bad attitude, worse than most.

Physical Oddness: Good heavens! The man has a pig for a foot! You almost can't blame him for becoming a bad apple!

The Bad Plan: He tried to turn me into the world's biggest lightbulb, and then fry Arthur by floating him around it. Oh, the irony! And he also wanted to do it on TV! Can TV actually be used as a device for evil?

The Ottoman

Evil Powers: The Ottoman commands all that is furniture. And just look around you. Furniture is everywhere!

Physical Oddness: There is nothing really odd about The Ottoman, except that she fell in love with Die Fledermaus.

The Bad Plan: The Ottoman wanted to marry Die Fledermaus and together they would terrorize The City in a horrible crime wave. It's one thing to be evil yourself, but to try and corrupt a superhero, even if he's a mediocre hero— that's just going too far, especially on the first date.

MIGHTY BLUE JUST

The Fin

Evil Powers: The Fin possesses an evil-genius brain. And it's not just an ordinary evil-genius brain, it's an evil-genius DOLPHIN brain!

Physical Oddness: He is the world's smartest dolphin, and he can talk. And not just that regular dolphin-chatter that we all love, but an actual command of the English language.

The Bad Plan: The Fin, who was formerly the performing dolphin Mr. Smarty-Pants, created a giant fish magnet. And who knew that fishes could be attracted by magnets. I didn't, but The Fin did.

The Human Ton and Handy

Evil Powers: He's really strong and really heavy. He's 2,000 pounds of nasty evil. And he talks to Handy, the puppet on his hand. The puppet alone is bad enough, but get these two together and look out! It's an all-evil slumber party.

Physical Oddness: He's 2,000 pounds of nasty evil. The puppet is creepy looking, too.

The Bad Plan: He tried to eat my head once. He also tends to work with this century's greatest criminal mastermind, The Terror. I think Handy likes to read, which is a fine thing for all boys and girls to do, but just plain twisted for a hand puppet to do!

The Red Herring

Evil Powers: The Red Herring is coated in petroleum jelly and is slimey like a fish! He's also got guns for eyes.

Physical Oddness: That's sure one freaky-weird costume he wears.

The Bad Plan: He is really Milton Rowe, fishmonger and international jewel thief.

Whirlin' Scottish Devil

Evil Powers: He spins and steals. Spin, spin, spin! Steal, steal, steal!

Physical Oddness: Kilt!

The Ead Plan: I don't know too much about this guy. I just knocked a statue's head on top of him on my return from outer space. But everyone seemed to think this was a good thing.

The Heys

Evil Powers: As evil space aliens, they have all the powers that evil space aliens possess.

Physical Oddness: The Heys all look just like Arthur, which may not be overly weird to them, but was just plain freaky for me.

The Bad Plan: Like most evil space aliens, they followed the typical evil space alien plan: they wanted to destroy the universe! Why do they always want to do that?

MIGHTY BLUE JUSTICE!

Special Agent Jim Rave

Evil Powers: He really has none. He's just a dork.

Physical Oddness: Well, he has an eye patch, but two perfectly working eyes! He just wants to be cool.

The Bad Plan: He spent twenty years trying to destroy a mustache. What a loser.

Indigestible Man

Evil Powers: No amount of stomach acid, no matter how strong, can digest the Indigestible Man.

Physical Oddness: The fact that he's made a career of allowing himself to be swallowed so he can swim around inside people. That's pretty darn gross.

The Bad Plan: Indigestible Man is a free agent and works for any villain who needs his particularly disgusting skills. When I met up with this fiend, he was working for Chairface Chippendale.

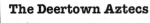

The Deertown Aztecs

Evil Powers: They don't actually have any powers, just a fierce devotion to pretending that they are real Aztecs. Although, their leader, Wally, does have a creepy glowing skull on the end of his baseball bat.

Physical Oddness: None, really. But they keep saying "Itlan" and that really gets on your nerves, man!

The Bad Plan: They wanted to kidnap Carmelita and marry her. I guess going after Carmelita isn't all that bad, but they nabbed Arthur instead.

THE CATALOGUE OF VILLAINY

Baron Violent

Evil Powers: Baron Violent possesses a special belt that makes you get stronger and stronger and stronger. Not only that, it just makes you plain nasty and bad... even when someone who is all around nice and good wears it—like Arthur.

Physical Oddness: Hey! He's just a little guy!

The Bad Plan: It seems that Baron Violent just wants to wreck stuff and fight for no real reason, except that he can. Random acts of injustice are right on the bottom of my list, let me tell you! Right down there with eating kittens.

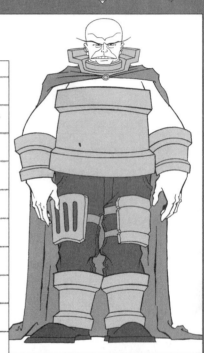

SewerCzar, Czar of the Sewers

Evil Powers: SewerCzar has the evil recipe to create a yucky army of sewer-beings called Filth. They carry out all his grimy commands.

Physical Oddness: Well, the guy lives in the sewers. And living in the sewers doesn't only stink with evil, it just plain stinks!

The Bad Plan: SewerCzar is the arch-enemy of none other than Sewer Urchin. Pretty convenient, eh? Sewer Urchin told me that SewerCzar was originally Lou Salizar, the most despicable civil servant in the history of solid-waste management. With his unlimited army of Filth, he plans to seek revenge by clogging the kitchens and bathrooms of The City.

Filth

Evil Powers: Filth are creatures made of pure yucky, grimy sewage. They have the power to be all mushy and flow through the pipes of the sewers, and man, they're mighty stinky, too!

Physical Oddness: All the Filth guys, despite being pure-ugly, are possibly the squishiest force of evil I've ever encountered.

The Bad Plan: Filth carry out the dirty orders of SewerCzar, the Czar of the Sewers. Being kind of dim creatures, the evil they cause isn't really their fault. But no time for pity! Remember, if you encounter one of these beasts, a bar of soap is your best defense!

MIGHTY BLUE JUSTICE!

Octo Paginini

Evil Powers: He's one of these evil-genius types, and is known throughout Europe as the "Virtuoso of Villainy" and the "Maestro of Malevolence."

Physical Oddness: The guy has six arms, which you might think is odd enough, but it's worse than just that. He doesn't stop playing his violins. Ever!

The Bad Plan: Paginini planned to kidnap the King of Belgium and replace him with a robot double. Then, Paginini (somehow) would rule all of Belgium. But really—Belgium? What's the big deal?

Eastern Bloc Robot Cowboy

Evil Powers: Eastern Bloc Robot Cowboy is a genius in robotics and uses these smarts not to build cute robots that do your laundry and wear little tin aprons, but to build evil robots! And evil robots wear nothing but bad intentions!

Physical Oddness: Well, isn't it obvious, chum? The man's a vending machine, with a brain where all the yummy soda should be. And he wears a cowboy hat. I mean, c'mon!

The Bad Plan: While helping out the evil Octo Paginini, he designed and created a robot double of the King of Belgium.

THE CATALOGUE OF VILLAINY

PART 4: ARTHUR'S PART OF THE BOOK FILLED WITH SCIENTIFIC INTEREST AND AMAZING FACTS, QUALIFYING THIS BOOK AS "EDUCATIONAL" SO THAT IT WILL BE OKAY TO READ IT IN SCHOOLS!

There is a lot of information in this book telling you the nifty ins and outs of being a superhero. But the learning can't stop there. To be a good superhero, you need to know all sorts of things. I've asked Arthur, who is just about the smartest person I know, to write down some smart things. So now if you get any grief from a licensed paid educator because you are reading this book in your school or postsecondary institution, you quickly flip to this section and proudly hold it up and yell, "Look at me! I'm getting book smarts!"

The Lunar Gods

The Moon has been precious to humankind since the dawn of civilization. In the earliest cultures, the Moon was worshiped under many names: Hecate, Diana, and Astarte. The first farmers timed the sowing and reaping of their crops by the phases of the ancient Moon. Lovers, poets, philosophers, and dreamers have always looked to the Moon for inspiration.

Hay Fever

Hay fever is an allergic response to airborne pollen. The symptoms can include itchy nose and throat, eyes, tearing, a clear nasal discharge, and terrible sneezing.

MIGHTY BLUE JUSTICE!

The Internal-Combustion Engine

The internal-combustion engine, perfected by Nikolaus August Otto in the last half of the nineteenth century, runs on a carefully controlled mixture of gasoline and air. The mixture is fed into a cylinder and ignited by a spark plug. This causes a small explosion that drives the piston, creating the movement of the engine. The choke valve controls how much air enters the fuel mixture. Without air, the fuel cannot ignite and floods the engine, causing it to stall.

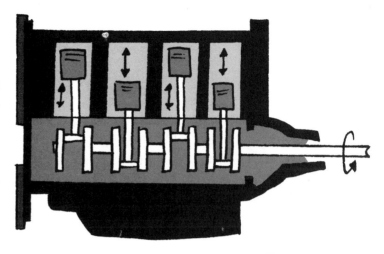

The Sound Barrier

Discovered by Chuck Yeager, the first man to achieve level flight at Mach-1 speed (the speed of sound), the sonic boom is a violently loud noise. It is caused by the shock wave generated by an aircraft flying

CHUCK YEAGER

MIDNIGHT BOMBER SEZ:
"I SAYS, 'SURF'S UP SPACE PONIES! I'M MAKING GRAVY WITHOUT THE LUMPS!'"

ARTHUR'S PART OF THE BOOK FILLED WITH SCIENTIFIC INTEREST AND AMAZING FACTS

faster than the speed of sound. Though not harmful to humans or animals, the sonic boom can be, on some occasions, loud enough to shatter glass.

Aspirin

Nearly two thousand years ago a brew made from white willow leaves was recommended for gout. Today, a remedy based on that same chemical, aspirin, is the most widely used medicine in the world. But aspirin is strong medicine, and should be taken only as directed. And children should never, ever, take aspirin, except under the supervision of their parents or a licensed physician.

Nikola Tesla

The brilliant inventor and electrical engineer Nikola Tesla developed the alternating-current (AC) power system that provides electricity for homes and buildings. Tesla was granted more than 100 United States' patents. Many of his discoveries led to electronic developments for which other scientists were honored. Tesla had laid the theoretical basis for radio communication as early as 1892; Guglielmo Marconi claimed all basic radio patents because of his own pioneering work in the field. In 1915 Tesla made an unsuccessful attempt to obtain a court

MIGHTY BLUE JUSTICE!

injunction against the claims of Marconi. When the United States Supreme Court reviewed this decision in 1943, however, it reversed the decision and invalidated Marconi's patents on the grounds that they had indeed been anticipated by earlier work. During his later years Tesla led a secluded, eccentric, and often destitute life, nearly forgotten by the world he believed would someday honor him. Tesla died on Jan. 7, 1943, in New York City. The Tesla Museum in Belgrade, Yugoslavia, was dedicated to the inventor. In 1956 the tesla, a unit of magnetic flux density in the metric system, was named in his honor.

ARTHUR'S PART OF THE BOOK FILLED WITH SCIENTIFIC INTEREST AND AMAZING FACTS

PART 5: THE TICK'S STUFF

This is my collection of stuff I've collected from my past adventures. Fabulous souvenirs, informative and colorful brochures, and stuff Arthur let me cut out of newspapers! Swell! You also get a look at "Arthur's Casebook." The little soldier has been keeping fabulous notes on all our adventures. What a smart cookie!

Arthur's Casebook

I'm keeping this journal to record all my super heroic exploits and adventures—if I can find some. I decided that I needed to finally express myself as who I am, and go with the life the moth suit will (hopefully) bring me. I was also fired from my accounting job today. I hope everything works out.

I met The Tick today. He promised me that he can lead me on the path to adventure. I saw him fall off a building and get up, so I kind of believe him. Right after I met him we came across The Idea Men, some villains who were robbing the Rive Droite Bank. The Tick managed to stop The Idea Men, but they got away in their blimp. This was my first taste of crime fighting. I trust The Tick. I'm going to let him stay at my place for a while. I hope he doesn't break anything, or do anything goofy.

Next, The Idea Men announced that they were going to blow up The City dam, unless they were paid ten million dollars. The Tick and I rushed to the scene, but when we ran out of rooftops to jump across, we had to take a cab (that I had to pay for). When we got to the dam, we found out The Idea Men were going to blow up the dam, even though they got their ransom. The Tick found their bomb, and in his attempt to "defuse" it, managed to save the dam and destroy The Idea Men's blimp.

Arthur's Casebook

While out on patrol, The Tick and I came across a group of criminals stealing a great big crate from the Superweapons Laboratory. We engaged them in a fight and were doing pretty good... until The Tick got a ladder wrapped around his head.

Luckily, American Maid showed up, and we managed to beat the bad guys, except one got away. She got pretty mad at us because she had been staking out these guys, in hopes of finding out who their ringleader was. I found a birthday card on one of the unconscious felons, indicating they were working for Chairface Chippendale! The Tick volunteered us to help American Maid infiltrate Chairface's hideout and help her stop the crime of the century! She had us dress as caterers so we could crash the birthday party. When we got there, The Tick and I served crab puffs. There were a lot of scary guys there, and with such appalling manners! Our cover was blown pretty quickly, and Chairface captured us and dangled us over man-eating alligators! One of them actually ate my tie! Then Chairface revealed to us his evil plot: The Awesome Giesmann Heat Ray, with which he planned to write his name upon the face of the Moon. While Chairface talked, The Tick got us away from the alligators by pulling us out with his teeth. Then The Tick and American Maid argued about how to stop Chairface, as he managed to write the letters C, H, and A on the Moon, so I took it upon myself to stop him by simply turning off the heat ray. Unfortunately, Chairface caught me, but in came The Tick and American Maid. While they took on the crowd, I faced off against Professor Chromedome. I blinded him with a flashlight, and gained control of the heat ray, which we pointed at Chairface. He gave up, but vowed revenge. When it was all over, American Maid actually said it was good working with us. Maybe this superhero thing is going to work, after all!

THE TICK CATERS TO NO MAN!

80

MIGHTY BLUE JUSTICE!

A HEART OF GOLD BEATS BENEATH THAT BIG FIBERGLASS CROISSANT - AND THANK GOODNESS FOR IT!

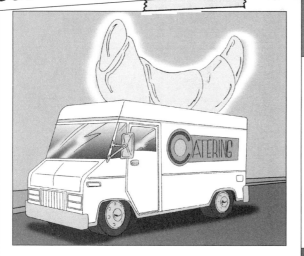

Happy Birthday to me!
You are cordially invited to a
birthday party for the world's
greatest criminal mastermind.
Gift required. Come see me commit the most
daring, spectacular crime of this,
or any other, century! R.S.V.P.

Vandalism: Has It Gone Too Far?

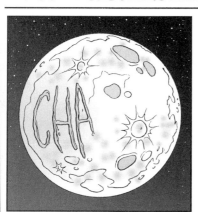

Evil criminal mastermind Chairface Chippendale tried to commit the crime of the century this weekend, by using a stolen experimental heat ray, the Giesmann Heat Ray, to write his name across the face of the Moon. Superheroes American Maid, The Tick, and an unidentified man dressed like a bunny thwarted Chairface Chippendale's scheme, but not in time to stop him from writing the letters "CHA" (as seen in photo) upon the surface of the Moon.

Scientists from the National Space Agency said today that they are looking into the situation, and efforts to repair the Moon could be made within a year, depending on a viable plan to erase letters that are hundreds of miles away.

THE TICK'S STUFF 81

Arthur's Casebook

The Tick and I took morning patrol off to go to Dinosaur Grotto. There we met Dinosaur Neil, who showed us his experemental attempt to grow dinosaurs from dinosaur DNA. But

Dinosaur Neil got his pasta salad and

> **HE HAS THE MUSTACHE OF A TITAN!**

his dinosaur tissue sample mixed up, and ate the tissue sample. That caused Dinosaur Neil to turn into a giant rampaging dinosaur, who started destroying The City! I remembered something that Dinosaur Neil told us in the lab—that he kept the dinosaur tissue in a solution of acetylsalicylic acid to keep it from growing. And knowing that acetylsalicylic acid is more commonly know as aspirin, The Tick and I went and got a giant aspirin to give to Dinosaur Neil. The Tick took the giant pill and jumped into Dinosaur Neil's mouth, to try to throw the pill into Dinosaur Neil's stomach. For a while, we didn't know if Dinosaur Neil had actually eaten The Tick, and I had to stop the National Guard from using all their tanks to stop Neil. It turned out that The Tick had to fight with Dinosaur Neil's tongue, and actually put it into a stranglehold to knock it out, before he could throw the pill into Neil's stomach. The Tick managed to escape, although he was covered in saliva (ick), and Dinosaur Neil turned back to his normal size.

> WELL, ONCE AGAIN, MY FRIEND, WE FIND THAT SCIENCE IS A TWO-HEADED BEAST. ONE HEAD IS NICE, IT GIVES US ASPIRIN AND OTHER MODERN CONVENIENCES... BUT THE OTHER HEAD OF SCIENCE IS BAD! OH, BEWARE THE OTHER HEAD OF SCIENCE, ARTHUR, IT BITES!

MIGHTY BLUE JUSTICE!

Sally Vacuum: Good evening, I'm Sally Vacuum. The authorities have issued a citywide alert: Dinosaur Neil, head paleontologist and tour guide at Dinosaur Grotto, is now seventy feet tall and walking down Main Street. As you can see, Dinosaur Neil is still growing, and no one knows where it will end! We have with us one of The City's superheroes, Die Fledermaus.
Die Fledermaus: Thank you, Sally.
Sally Vacuum: Die Fledermaus, can you tell us what the super-hero community plans to do about this menace?
Die Fledermaus: Good question, Sally. Actually, I think we'll just sit it out and wait for the National Guard.
Sally Vacuum: This has been Sally Vacuum at the scene of the "Dinosaur Neil Crisis."
Die Fledermaus: So... when's this going to be on?

Sally Vacuum: Once again, this is Sally Vacuum at the scene of the "Dinosaur Neil Crisis." The National Guard does have the deranged dinosaur surrounded but maintains a tense cease-fire. Apparently one of The City's most prominent superheroes, The Tick, has fed himself to Dinosaur Neil along with an enormous aspirin, in a desperate attempt to bring the rampaging reptile under control. The Tick appears to have been devoured in one of the most selfless and heroic acts this reporter has ever witnessed. This, after a spokesman for the superhero community said that they would "sit it out, and wait for the National Guard." Minutes ago, I recorded an exclusive interview with the pharmacist who provided the giant aspirin that may be the key to the dinosaur's downfall.
Sally Vacuum: That was quite an aspirin.
Sid: Oh, I suppose so.
Sally Vacuum: Was that the largest prescription that you have ever filled?
Sid: Oh, yes. But I made a huge cough drop once.
Sally Vacuum: And how big was that?
Sid: About the size of a quarter.
Sally Vacuum: Thank you, Sid the pharmacist.
There is a solemn silence at the Must-Go-Shopping Plaza as we all wait to see what fate has befallen The Tick.

HEY KIDS! COME TO DINOSAUR GROTTO!

★ COME FOR DAILY GUIDED TOURS OF A WORKING DINOSAUR DIG!

★ COME WATCH OUR TEAM OF EXPERT SCIENTISTS DIG UP REAL DINOSAUR BONES!

★ ENJOY HIGH QUALITY SOUVENIRS AT OUR FABULOUS GIFT SHOP!

★ TAKE FULL ADVANTAGE OF OUR AMPLE PARKING LOT!

★ OUR DINOSAUR SNACK BAR VOTED "BEST FRIES AND GRAVY CONCESSION STAND IN THE TRI-STATE AREA!"

ASK ABOUT OUR FUN DINOSAUR BIRTHDAY PARTIES!

"COME AND SEE THESE GIANT REPTILES THAT RULED PREHISTORIC EARTH FOR EONS. THEY WEREN'T VERY BRIGHT, BUT THEY WERE VERY, VERY BIG!" - DINOSAUR NEIL CHIEF PALEONTOLOGIST

MEET OUR CHIEF PALEONTOLOGIST, *DINOSAUR NEIL*. HE'S ALWAYS HAPPY TO ANSWER ANY OF YOUR QUESTIONS AND HELP YOU IN ANY WAY.

REMEMBER, *OUR GIFT SHOP* OFFERS EVERYTHING FOR YOUR *MERCHANDISE* AND *CONSUMER NEEDS!*

To Dinosaur Grotto:
Take Route 9 to Highway 5, and head west for 3 miles, then head north until you reach Bissette Road, and follow the signs to Dinosaur Grotto! Parking is on the south side.

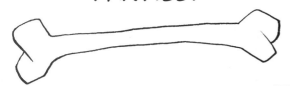

Pants On Fire!

Disaster struck as lightning hit the giant pants intended to contain the rampaging Dinosaur Neil, setting the trousers ablaze.

THE TICK'S STUFF

Arthur's Casebook

The Tick and I were invited to a free evening out at the Evil Eye Cafe. I didn't think it was such a good idea to go, but we went, and Mr. Mental, who was posing as a harmless mentalist with a hypnotist act, hypnotized The Tick. But he must have done more than make The Tick cluck like a chicken because that night The Tick got up and busted out of the apartment. I followed him as he leapt from roof to roof, but I couldn't stop him. Finally The Tick snapped out of it and told me that he was dreaming Mr. Mental was giving him directions, and that he should "go for a swim." I went and found Die Fledermaus, Crusading Chameleon, and Sewer Urchin. The four of us couldn't find The Tick anywhere, and Sewer Urchin even searched underwater for us. It turned out that Mr. Mental hypnotised The Tick to break in to the Pendecker Laboratory and steal the experimental Thinking Cap. When we found The Tick on his way back from the lab, Sewer Urchin, Crusading Chameleon, and I couldn't stop him (Die Fledermaus didn't even try and just went home), but we did follow The Tick to Mr. Mental. With the Thinking Cap on, Mr. Mental could do all sorts of things, like fly and levitate objects. Seeing that the Thinking Cap ran with an internal-combustion engine, I realized that if we were to pull the choke on the engine, it would flood Mr. Mental's mind! After a big fight with Mr. Mental, The Tick managed to get close enough to Mr. Mental and, resisting his eye beam blasts, was able to pull the choke, resulting in Mr. Mental's defeat.

> THE NIGHT IS YOUNG AND WE HAVE UMBRELLAS IN OUR DRINKS.

> A DAY JOB... IN AN OFFICE? MY WORST NIGHTMARE!

MIGHTY BLUE JUSTIC

> You are invited.
> A Night to Remember.
> "The Evil Eye"
> FREE!

Thinking Cap Stolen from Pendecker Laboratory.
Mysterious Sea-Monster Responsible!

Captured by a security camera, it is plain to see the hideous swamp-beast fighting the laboratory's security robot. Exactly why such a foul beast would want the Thinking Cap, a high-tech, experimental device that increases a normal person's mental, telepathic, and telekinetic abilities, is unknown. Chief researchers at the Pendecker Laboratory said today that the Thinking Cap's one major drawback is that if in the hands of a super villain, "It could easily be used for evil."

> THE HUMAN MIND IS A DANGEROUS PLAYTHING, BOYS. WHEN IT'S USED FOR EVIL, WATCH OUT! BUT WHEN IT'S USED FOR GOOD, THEN THINGS ARE MUCH NICER.

"DIDN'T FIND THE TICK, BUT I FOUND A BEAUTIFUL PIE."

HERE'S AN EXCELLENT TIME TO GO BACK AND CHECK OUT PART FOUR AND READ UP ON THE MIGHTY FORCE OF THE SONIC BOOM!

Arthur's Casebook

While out on "patrol" at Stuart's Food Castle, The Tick and I were present for the explosion of a "bread bomb" from The Breadmaster. When the bomb went off, the supermarket filled with expanding bread, consuming The Tick. I created an impromptu life preserver from an oversized plastic donut and pulled The Tick, and a puppy, out of the growing bread. Stuart's Food Castle was unfortunately destroyed, but The Tick managed to save a box of cotton swabs, which is good, I guess. On a later patrol we came across another bread bomb destroying the Whitebread Baking Company. Deducing that could get some information about evil bakers there, we headed to the City Baking College, where the dean told us of one student who was expelled for "pursuing perverse baking experiments."

While there, a bread-bomb warning was phoned in by The Breadmaster. We found the bread bomb in the basement, and The Tick managed to defuse it by eating the bomb into submission. Next, The Breadmaster made a demand for large quantities of baking supplies, and when he came to pick up the sugar, we ambushed him. The Breadmaster threw a giant dinner roll, and Buttery Pat helped The Breadmaster make his escape. I used my wings to cut The Tick and me free from the giant roll. Fortunately, in his rushed getaway, The Breadmaster left behind his recipe for a killer soufflé, and we tracked him to the Municipal Swimming Pool, where he was mixing up his next plan. The Tick and I got there in time to stop The Breadmaster, but not in time to stop the soufflé. I figured out that we needed to create a giant sonic boom to destroy the growing soufflé before it crushed The City. We called upon The Human Bullet to shoot The Tick at the giant soufflé, causing a sonic boom that destroyed the soufflé and saved The City.

Sally Vacuum: A new super villain has descended upon The City again, calling himself The Breadmaster, and this so-called Breadmaster has issued an ultimatum to Mayor Blank. He's demanded common baking ingredients in enormous quantities. And if they are not delivered per his instructions, he will escalate his "bread bombings." Mayor Blank announced his decision at a press conference earlier today.

Mayor Blank: I have okayed the delivery of the supplies The Breadmaster demands.

Reporter: But, Your Honor, isn't it The City's policy to refuse all terrorist demands?

Mayor Blank: Well... yes... I suppose you could call these terrorist acts. But they're also acts of baking. Very fast, big baking.

NOT BAKED GOODS, PROFESSOR; BAKED BADS!

SO WARM... SO SOFT... COULD SLEEP FOREVER. NO! MUST FIGHT, MUSTN'T SUCCUMB TO THE RAPTURE OF THE BREAD!

YEAST DEVIL! BACK TO THE OVEN THAT BAKED YOU!

I'M BETTING THAT I'M JUST ABNORMAL ENOUGH TO SURVIVE.

City-Smothering Lemon Soufflé recipe

2,000 cubic feet whole milk

yolks of 30,000 gross of eggs

6 tons granulated sugar

4 tons fresh flour

2 tons lemon juice

756 lbs. grated lemon rind

whites of 50,000 gross of eggs

one boxcar confectioners' sugar for dusting <optional>

1. Set aside 750 cubic feet of milk

LET US NOT FORGET THE LESSON THAT WE CAN LEARN FROM THIS, ARTHUR, THAT MAN WAS NOT MEANT TO TAMPER WITH THE FOUR BASIC FOOD GROUPS.

THE TICK'S STUFF

Arthur's Casebook

While at Angry Hank's Fat Pig Barbecue, The Tick and I found the cacti to be a little... rambunctious. We fought off the attacks of the cacti, and discovered that all over The City plants were turning violent. Later, while on patrol, we were buzzed by a plane crop dusting the City Park. Just then, the trees started misbehaving, so The Tick managed to leap onto the plane, and found the evil villain, El Seed, at the controls. In the scuffle on the plane, a beaker of El Seed's chemical spilled all over The Tick. He fell off the plane, and we found ourselves surrounded by agitated trees in the park. The Tick was really, really disoriented; more so than usual! He was all glowing, and green, and then flowers and potatoes started growing out of him. After The Civic Minded Five took care of the rampaging trees, I took The Tick to the emergency room. By this time, The Tick was sprouting grass! The doctor decided that the solution to The Tick's problem was expensive testing. The test results told us The Tick had twelve hours before he completely turned into a vegetable! The Tick figured that El Seed had to have an antidote. We tracked El Seed to Jeff's Pay & Spray Crop Duster Rentals. Jeff was able to tell us that El Seed was at the Old Abandoned Greenhouse. We walked down the road to get there (and it was quite a ways away), but before long, El Seed buzzed us with the plane and dropped his chemical on a cornfield, causing the corn to become very unfriendly toward us. The Tick was able to grow corn out of his body, which helped us blend in, and we were able to infiltrate the corn army. We managed to get in to the Abandoned Greenhouse, and got the antidote with just thirty seconds to spare! The Tick was saved! I also figured that we could use the crop duster to drop the antidote onto the corn army, too. The corn turned back into normal law-abiding vegetables, and The Civic Minded Five put El Seed under citizens' arrest. All the plants, everywhere, turned back to normal. I think.

> VILLAINS ALWAYS HAVE ANTIDOTES... THEY'RE FUNNY THAT WAY.

> I HATE BROCCOLI, AND YET, IN A CERTAIN SENSE, I AM BROCCOLI.

> LIFE IS A BIG WILD CRAZY TOSSED SALAD, BUT YOU DON'T EAT IT, NO, SIR! YOU LIVE IT! ISN'T IT GREAT?

Sally Vacuum: That was the scene late today, when a strange tree riot broke out in the City Park. A surprisingly brave handful of our City's superheroes fought through the day and saved park goers and finally subdued the dangerous greenery. Many of the heroes were brought to the City Hospital with minor injuries and severe splinters. More after this.

Angry Trees Attack Park!

"I didn't want to be involved. I got jumped by a hedge. Where are the cops in this town?"

86 CHA

MIGHTY BLUE JUSTICE!

OUR I.D. CARDS:

the TICK
(superhero)

SUPERHERO

DIE FLEDERMAUS

OFFICIAL SUPERHERO IDENTIFICATION CARD

Sewer Urchin

I GET IT, SPELLING AMERICA WITH A "K", ARE WE?

YEAH, WELL, DON'T COUNT YOUR WEASELS BEFORE THEY POP, DINK!

CAN'T LOSE MY NAME, IT'S ON ALL MY STATIONERY!

Arthur's Casebook:

The Tick wanted me to take him and Die Fledermaus and Sewer Urchin to some crazy superhero nightclub in the middle of nowhere. When we got to the place, the Comet Club, the doorman, Doorman, wouldn't let me in because I was a sidekick. No sidekicks were allowed in the club—they had to go to the Sidekick's Lounge out back; the Sidekick's Lounge was really lame. I went into the bathroom, which also went into the Comet Club. There was this crazy little man in there who was carrying a bag with the word "bombs" on it. When I asked him about it, he yelled, "I'm The Evil Midnight Bomber What Bombs at Midnight!" and threw a smoke bomb at me! Of course, I got out of there and went into the Comet Club to get someone to help stop the Midnight Bomber. Before I could, I was grabbed by Doorman. And also, The Tick was fighting Barry/The Tick. Doorman wouldn't listen to me. Fortunately, Sewer Urchin helped me and stunk Doorman into unconsciousness, and I was able to get into the club and get The Tick. The Tick and I only had twenty seconds to get all the bombs out of the club. We managed to do it, but the Sidekick's Lounge kind of suffered for it. The Tick still had to deal with this Barry/Tick guy, and I chased down The Evil Midnight Bomber. Even though we managed to catch a super villain, it was still a pretty lousy night out.

THE TICK'S STUFF

HEY, BOYS AND TALKING ANIMALS!!!
THE OFFICIAL SIDEKICK'S LOUNGE NEWS 'N' GAMES BOOK

Spring/Summer issue
A fine booklet published in association with the Comet Club to entertain and inform the young minds of today's top sidekicks!

SIDEKICK'S

LOUNGE

Exclusive this issue: Johnny Omega's tips for reducing **"spandex itch"!**

MIDNIGHT BOMBER SEZ: "AND SO HE SAYS TO ME, 'YOU WANNA BE A BAD GUY?' AND I SAYS 'YEAH, BABY! I WANNA BE BAD!'"

Member of the Electricity Club, the Speech-Making Club, the Clock Club, the Chemistry Club. Founder and president of the Caffeine and Sleep-Deprivation Club and the short-lived "I Grok Evil" Club. Voted "Most Likely to Be Alienated From Society."

In memory of **Johnny Republic.**

So long, **Johnny Wingless.**

Memorial to **Johnny Fathom.**

MIGHTY BLUE JUSTICE!

SO, FOUL
GELATIN, YOU
WOULD DO
BATTLE WITH
THE NOSE OF
YOUR BIRTH?

DON'T

Dr. Thrakk's
Secret Cloning
Sauce
(generous helping)
- A pinch of
oregano
- Tissue sample
(from a hair, toe-
nail, or any
genetic sample
available)
- Mix well in
Clonerizer, then
serve. Clone is
immediately ready
to receive
orders.

I DON'T KNOW THE
MEANING OF THE
WORD SURREN-
DER! I MEAN, I
KNOW IT, I'M NOT
DUMB... JUST NOT
IN THIS CONTEXT.

Arthur's Casebook:

The Tick caught a cold, which of itself was more work for me than any super villain. While taking care of Tick, what seemed like improperly delivered mail arrived at the apartment. I went to take it back to apt. 14B, but when I did I was abducted by Thrakkorzog, an evil ambeoid ruler from dimension 14B! Thrakkorzog told me of his plan to clone The Tick and create an army of them to do his bidding. To create a Tick clone, he needed a tissue sample, and so he created a clone of me to attain the tissue sample. I didn't think The Tick would be fooled by the pathetic clone of me, which just walked around saying, "I Arthur..." But he was. I managed to escape from Thrakkorzog after I tricked his weird roommate into loosening the straps that Thrakkorzog tied me up with. I was able to get back to our apartment, to help The Tick just as the Arthur-Clone was making his move. But during my fight with the clone, The Tick couldn't tell which one of us was the real Arthur. Only after the clone's head exploded with tentacles and wiggling eyeballs was The Tick convinced I was the real Arthur. But it was too late. Thrakkorzog had enough time to create a horrible Tick-Clone, made from one of The Tick's used tissues (ick!). Thrakkorzog's roommate didn't want us to fight in the apartment, or they might lose their deposit, so we all went up to the roof, and there The Tick started his fight with the Evil Mucus-Tick. I came up with a plan, remembering a machine in Thrakkorzog's apartment could send Thrakkorzog back to his own dimension. I went to get it and take it back to the roof. It was really heavy, and it needed an extension cord! By the time I got everything together, The Tick looked like he was in a bit of trouble, but I gave him the "high-sign," and The Tick was able to suck the Evil Mucus-Tick into his sinuses. I pressed the "DON'T" button, and Tick sneezed the clone and Thrakkorzog into the dimensional portal that was created. At the end of it all, The Tick was feeling better, but it looked like I had picked up his cold.

MUCAL
INVADER, IS
THERE NO
END TO YOUR
OOZING?!

THE TICK'S STUFF

89
CHA

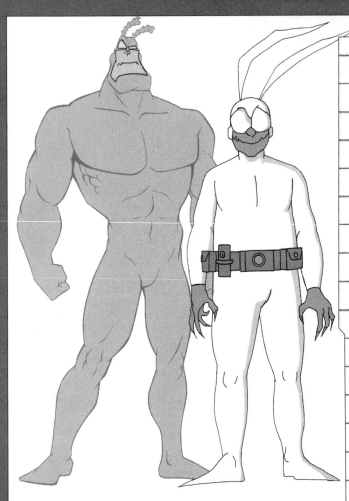

How to Spot an Evil Clone

Clones are wily creatures with the power to deceive! Don't feel bad if you miss spotting a clone. It's not hard to do. So here's some tips to help everyone spot an evil clone.

1. Clones often have an odd skin tone. In this instance, the clone's was green. Green isn't an odd color, in itself. Many good things are green, like leafy trees and shrubs. But when your sidekick is green... look out!

2. Abnormal speech. Try engaging a suspected clone in conversation. If they can't cut you the straight facts, man, be careful! Talk about trivia, movies, or family. The answers might tell you if you are dealing with a clone or not.

3. The use of frightening weapons that the person doesn't normally use. There are certain things that only an evil clone would use, like devices to cut your head off!

4. Clones can do unusual things, like make eyeballs come out their ears! If your clone suspect is doing something physically full-on weird, then you've probably got a clone on your hands.

5. Clones have a "things are just not right" quality to them. Trust your instincts!

6. Unwholesome goals. Clones only want to achieve their slanted plans, like world conquest and the sinister urge to maim and hurt, and even kill. Remember, a true friend won't try to kill you.

DID YOU LEARN ENOUGH? IF NOT, GO BACK TO PAGE 76!

MIGHTY BLUE JUSTICE!

WORLD WACKY NEWS

Earthquakes! Tidal waves! The Moon falling out of orbit! The act of UFOs? Satan? Bigfoot?

No! It was the act of this twelve-year-old:
BRAINCHILD!

"Evil! Evil! I'm beside myself with evil!"
-Brainchild

He's got a robot dog! He's got a Mega-Devastator-Multi-Cannon! He doesn't make his bed!

He thinks up evil thoughts 24 hours a day! Inside: his top 10 evil thoughts, published for the very first time!

Arthur's Casebook:

While out at Angry Hank's buying a new microwave, we encountered a giant robot dog who seemed to be after the same microwave we wanted. As the robot dog made an escape, the toasters and other appliances attacked me. After The Tick defeated the appliances, we were able to track the robot dog to the home of Charles, the young super villain called Brainchild. After talking to the parents, The Tick tried to talk things out with the kid. It didn't really work. Brainchild sent out Skippy, the robot dog, to attack us, while he activated his Mega-Devastator-Multi-Cannon to smash the Moon into the Earth! Brainchild's parents tried (sort of) to talk their son out of crashing the Moon into the Earth, but decided that his urge to smash was just a natural step in his development. What flakes! We still had to deal with Skippy. In the scuffle, The Tick caused Skippy to crash into the Mega-Devastator-Multi-Cannon, which reversed it, returned the Moon to its proper place, and destroyed Brainchild's evil headquarters/tree house.

THE TICK'S STUFF

Arthur's Casebook:

One morning a group of secret government agents showed up and told us we were being sent to the island of Pokoponesia to rescue the space monkey Yank, who was exposed to cosmic rays and was now a super-genius, from Pokoponesia's evil dictator ruler Pineapple Pokopo. The government wanted Yank to head the National Space Program. We were recommended for this mission by American Maid, who was sort of leading the mission. We were given two-way wrist radios, too. We went to Pokoponesia "under cover," using the code names Jeanine, Arnie, and Nick. We found that Pokopo stays in a fortified palace on the north shore of the island, surrounded by deadly shark-infested waters. American Maid/Jeanine was invited to dinner by Pineapple Pokopo, so Tick/Nick and I headed to the palace. While I was moving through the jungle, a couple of Pokopo's henchmen grabbed me and tried to throw me off a cliff. They didn't believe our cover stories of us just being tourists. The Tick/Nick showed up, but they still tossed me off the cliff, to the sharks, after Tick/Nick told them "let him go!" I was able to activate my wings before I hit the water, and The Tick/Nick took care of the henchmen. With our cover now blown, we only had a short time to surf to the palace and avoid the projectile sharks before the henchmen could warn Pokopo. When we got to Pokopo's palace-fortress, American Maid had been captured and was about to be fed to the sharks. But we managed to rescue American Maid and get into the escape pod that Yank built. It turns out Pokopo wanted Yank to build him a weapon to destroy Hawaii, but instead he built the pod that rescued us all.

> LET'S HANG TEN FOR JUSTICE!

> YOU KNOW, GANG, WHEN YOU'RE A SUPERHERO, YOU NEVER KNOW WHERE THE DAY WILL TAKE YOU. YOU MAY FIND YOURSELF HALFWAY AROUND THE WORLD IN THE SHARK-INFESTED WATERS OF TRUE-TO-LIFE LIVING. OR YOU MAY FIND YOURSELF GOING DOWN TO THE STORE FOR A LOZENGE. YOU CAN'T KNOW, CAN YOU? NO! YOU GOTTA RIDE THAT WAVE, YOU GOTTA SUCK THAT LOZENGE! 'CAUSE IF YOU DON'T, WHO WILL?

78:14:30
- Elapsed orbital duration: seventy-eight hours fourteen minutes thirty seconds and counting.
- Subject vital signs: blood pressure: normal. Heart rate, respiration: good. Brain wave pattern: A-OK. It's feeding time.
- Activate automatic food-paste dispensal unit.
- Roger, FPDU is a go.
- Affirmative. We are blowing paste.
- He's eating it. We have a paste down.
- Congratulations, Houston.
- Roger, we are approaching Cosmic Ray Storm. Initiate emergency evasive... whoops, heh heh, spilled my coffee.
- Hey. Get some paper towels. Oh, I mean... uh... deploy, uhm... absorption panels.
- Central Tracking, continue to pat gently.
- Roger on the patting. I think we're seeing some progress.
- Oh yeah. That's coming out.
- Thank you, Houston, looks like we're out of the woods on that coffee stain.
- Ahem, uh... Houston? Uh, how's that monkey doing up there?
<Oh man.>
- Houston, was that you?
- Central Tracking, we didn't copy that.
<Copy this, you jerks. Get me down outta here.>
- Uh, Houston? That was the monkey.
- Roger, Central Tracking. We have talking monkey, and brain waves indicate "super-genius."
- Uh-oh.
<You clowns. What are you shooting monkeys into space for? Its been done to death.>
- Well, Yank, we just wanted to see what, ahem... what monkeys were like in space.
<I'll tell you what monkeys are like in space. Very angry.>
- And we're awful sorry, little buddy, but that Ray Storm blew out our remote guidance system. We can't get you down without it.
<Forget it. I'll get myself down, you dinks. But I'll see you in court.>

MIGHTY BLUE JUSTICE!

NSP to Launch Space Monkey

Early this morning, famed astronaut monkey Yank (seen above) was launched into space for what has become America's triumphant return of sending monkeys into orbit. "We were thinking of sending a dog, but hey, America loves monkeys!" said a National Space Program representative at a press conference in Houston yesterday.

But just why has the NSP turned their attention to such missions? "We think that sending monkeys into space is an excellent use of taxpayer money. The President likes it, NSP likes it and, quite frankly, America likes it. Heck, we're sure even the monkeys like it!" And with an outstanding approval rating like that, how can a simple journalist argue?

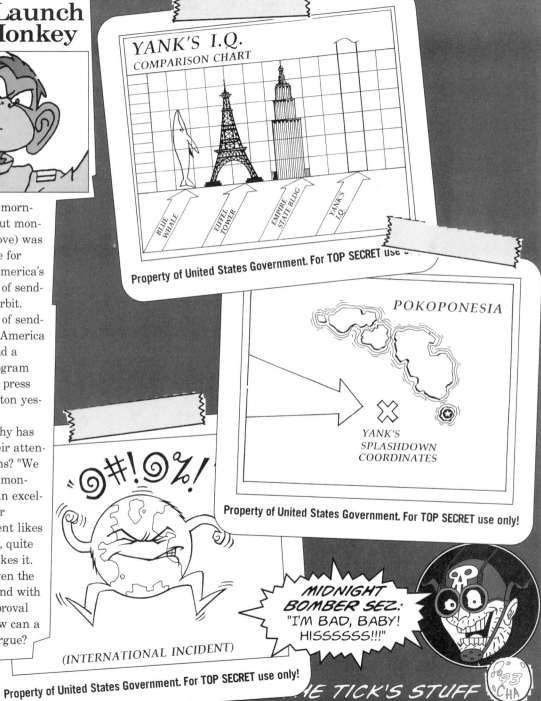

YANK'S I.Q. COMPARISON CHART

BLUE WHALE · EIFFEL TOWER · EMPIRE STATE BLDG · YANK'S I.Q.

Property of United States Government. For TOP SECRET use only!

POKOPONESIA

YANK'S SPLASHDOWN COORDINATES

Property of United States Government. For TOP SECRET use only!

"@#!@%!"

(INTERNATIONAL INCIDENT)

MIDNIGHT BOMBER SEZ: "I'M BAD, BABY! HISSSSSS!!!"

Property of United States Government. For TOP SECRET use only!

THE TICK'S STUFF

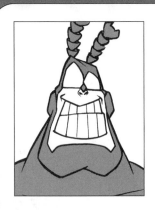

TEMPORARY SECRET
GOVERNMENT AGENT

The Tick

TOP SECRET
CLEARANCE - LEVEL
ORANGE

MIDNIGHT BOMBER SEZ: "HE SAYS TO ME, 'YOU GOTTA DO SOMETHING SMART, BABY! SOMETHING BIG!'"

TEMPORARY SECRET
GOVERNMENT AGENT

Arthur

TOP SECRET
CLEARANCE - LEVEL
ORANGE

PINEAPPLE AIR

SECRET CODE NAMES:

~~TOCK~~
~~TUCK~~
~~AAR. TUCK~~
~~AAR. TUCKER~~
~~TAB~~
~~TACK~~
~~JACK~~
~~TAD~~
~~DICK~~

NICK!!!!

CHECK OUT OUR KEEN UNDERCOVER GET UPS!

MIGHTY BLUE JUST

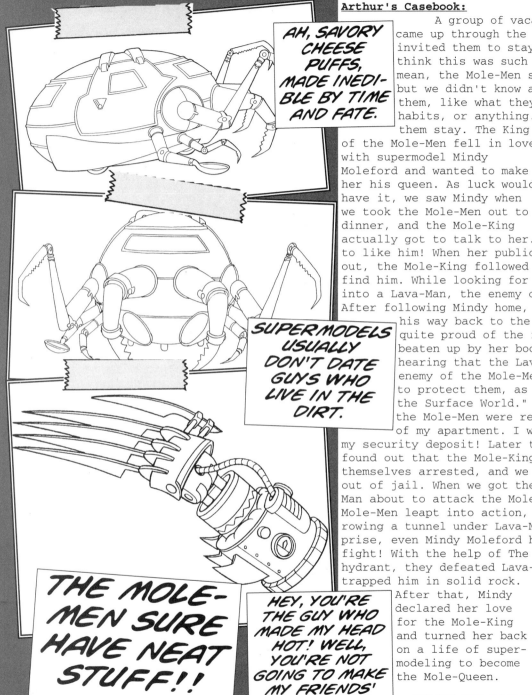

A group of vacationing Mole-Men came up through the basement, and Tick invited them to stay with us. I didn't think this was such a great idea. I mean, the Mole-Men seemed nice enough, but we didn't know anything about them, like what they eat, or their habits, or anything. Still... I let them stay. The King of the Mole-Men fell in love with supermodel Mindy Moleford and wanted to make her his queen. As luck would have it, we saw Mindy when we took the Mole-Men out to dinner, and the Mole-King actually got to talk to her. She even seemed to like him! When her publicist dragged her out, the Mole-King followed them. So we had to find him. While looking for him, The Tick ran into a Lava-Man, the enemy of the Mole-Men. After following Mindy home, Mole-King found his way back to the apartment. He was quite proud of the fact that he was beaten up by her bodyguards. Upon hearing that the Lava-Man was the enemy of the Mole-Men, The Tick swore to protect them, as "Ambassadors to the Surface World." I don't know, but the Mole-Men were really making a mess of my apartment. I was afraid of losing my security deposit! Later that night, we found out that the Mole-King and Larry got themselves arrested, and we had to bail them out of jail. When we got there we found Lava-Man about to attack the Mole-King. But the Mole-Men leapt into action, and started burrowing a tunnel under Lava-Man. To my surprise, even Mindy Moleford helped out in the fight! With the help of The Tick and a fire hydrant, they defeated Lava-Man and trapped him in solid rock. After that, Mindy declared her love for the Mole-King and turned her back on a life of supermodeling to become the Mole-Queen.

NOTE TO MYSELF: To get Tick to do some chores, call them "MISSIONS"!

THE TICK'S STUFF

The Ancient Traditional Mole-Man Courtship Ritual

Mindy!

(Mindy!)

Know now the bottomless pit that is my love for thee!

(Solid!)

Mindy! (Mindy!)

Join me in my subterranean palace!

(Cozy!)

Why live up here on the crust when you can be with me in the soily filling of the sweet earth pie?

(Better than it sounds!)

Mindy!

(Mindy!)

THE TICK'S STUFF

Arthur's Casebook:

On the way back from Wheatland, an amusement park devoted to grain, The Tick and I found The City deserted. The Civic Minded Five, Sewer Urchin, and Die Fledermaus showed up to tell us that every-one had been evacuated because of the threat of a large, angry clown called Proto-Clown! Tick tried to deal with Proto-Clown, but when he honked Proto-Clown's nose, and we all laughed, Proto-Clown hit The Tick so hard, he was launched into space! Without The Tick, we knew we were in big trouble. Fortunately, American Maid showed up with Doctor Bud Frontier, who was the scientist who created Proto-Clown. He tried to talk to Proto-Clown to get him to stop his rampage, but it didn't work. We decided to head back to The Civic Minded Five's headquarters, while American Maid and Die Fledermaus stayed behind to take on Proto-Clown. Back at The Civic-Minded Five's HQ (which was really nice—they had a pool table and nice wood paneling, and Feral Boy even had his own doggy door!), Dr. Frontier told us how he created Proto-Clown, figuring that if a normal clown was funny, then a giant clown would be funnier, and a theme park filled with giant clowns would be hilarious. Only one of his "Super Clowns" survived—Proto-Clown. Then American Maid and Die Fledermaus returned; it seemed Die Fledermaus had fainted. Unfortunately, Proto-Clown followed the two back to the headquarters. We ran to the garage. When Proto-Clown busted his way in, we finally found out why he was so angry: he didn't like being laughed at. Dr. Frontier promised to never laugh at Proto-Clown again, but then his nose honked again, and we couldn't help but laugh. Just as Proto-Clown was about to smash us all, The Tick fell from space right on top of Proto-Clown and knocked him out! Dr. Frontier vowed to take Proto-Clown back to his lab and try to make him less funny.

IT'S STARTING TO SMELL A LITTLE LIKE DANGER IN HERE, OR HEAVILY FRIED FOOD.

Announcer: The Mayor has issued a citywide alert! The Governor's office is expected to declare a state of emergency within an hour! As of this report, the entire municipal area has been evacuated. We are under attack (...STATIC...) thing so monstrous (...STAT-IC...) unleashed from the sacred, cotton candy place of our dreams. If anyone is out there listening, get out of town, before it gets to you! Get out now! Plea (...STATIC...) <end of broadcast>

WELL, ONCE AGAIN WE FIND THAT CLOWNING AND ANARCHY DON'T MIX.

WHILE OUT IN SPACE, I HAD TIME TO GET IN TOUCH WITH MY INNER SELF, GET TO KNOW MY PSYCHE, FIND OUT WHAT MAKES THE TICK TICK! THE MOST IMPORTANT THING WAS I WAS ABLE TO ASK ONE BIG QUESTION TO MY "SELF-IMAGE"...

HOW YA DOING???

SEE? CHECK IT OUT! THUMBS UP! EVERYTHING IS A-OK IN THE BRAIN OF THE TICK!

OH, WHAT A GOOFY WORK IS MAN!

MIGHTY BLUE JUSTICE!

Sally Vacuum: The City sleeps uneasily tonight as unconfirmed reports continue to trickle in. Apparently there have been several sightings—once again, unconfirmed—of the spidery steel mobile home belonging to the twentieth century's most notorious super villain, The Terror. The Terror, pictured here with infamous Soviet dictator Joseph Stalin, burst upon the super villain scene early in the summer of 1903 in a legendary fight with then President Theodore Roosevelt. This began an unparalleled career of epic wrongdoings: Paris, Lima, Deertown. No corner of the globe is safe from The Terror's reign of terror. Last sighted in 1976, The Terror, still holding a grudge, tried to punch out Mount Rushmore. Could The Terror be back? Tonight, a terrified City cringes in its collective pajamas. More as it develops.

Arthur's Casebook:

The Tick, spurred on by reports of the infamous super villain The Terror returning to The City, went nuts (well, more nuts than usual) and wanted to "upgrade" our "crime-busting equipment." The first thing he did was start construction on a "crime-busting tower." He also bought a real expensive-looking Tick-Signal for City Hall. Then he went and bought a pile of other "crime" junk that maxxed out my credit cards! That was the last straw! I had to kick him out! The Tick left, all right, but he went and sulked in his crime-busting tower. He wouldn't come out or fight crime or do anything. It was hopeless. Of course, this had to be the time that The Terror did show up and kidnap Mayor Blank. American Maid and I decided it was up to us to save the Mayor. While I created a diversion (okay, not my best diversion, but I was working under strained conditions), American Maid tried to rescue the Mayor, but he was too afraid to jump out the window. We needed help, and desperate times call for desperate measures, so I used the Tick-Signal that Tick gave the Mayor. To my great surprise, Tick snapped out of his funk! We fought The Terror's group of villains, which included The Human Ton and Handy, The Man-Eating Cow, Tuun-La, and a guy who looked like Stalin. After The Tick showed up, Tuun-La and the Stalin guy took off, Tick took on The Human Ton, American Maid captured The Terror, and I fought Handy (which was actually harder than you'd think). The battle was a success, and Tick and I made up.

YES, DESTINY HAS HER HAND ON MY BACK, AND SHE'S PUSHING!

EVIL, CHUM, IS EVER GREEN!

BUILD YOUR OWN CRIME BUSTING TOWER!

25 Complete instructions on following pages.

I CUT DOWN ON SOME OF THE BELLS AND WHISTLES THAT MADE THE MAGAZINE'S CRIME-BUSTING TOWER SO NEAT, BUT I THINK MY TOWER ISN'T WITHOUT IT'S OWN CHARM! ITS AMAZING WHAT WOOD, NAILS, AND A HAMMER WILL DO FOR YOU. WHY, THEY ARE EXACTLY THE ITEMS THAT THIS GREAT NATION IS BUILT UPON (ALTHOUGH, THERE MAY HAVE BEEN SOME STEEL AND IRON USED, TOO)!

MIGHTY BLUE JUSTICE!

Handy's Reading List

Becker, Ernest: *The Denial of Death*

Burgess, Anthony: *A Clockwork Orange*

Carroll, Lewis: *Alice's Adventures in Wonderland*

Cohen, Jason; Krugman, Michael; Dorkin, Evan: *Gene[...] The Backlash Starts Here*

Darwin, Charles: *On the Origin of Species by Means [...] Selection, or the Preservation of Favoured Races in [...] for Life*

Dickens, Charles: *A Tale of Two Cities*

Dylan, Bob: *Lyrics, 1962-1985 (selections)*

Far, Sui Sin: *A Love Story from the Rice Fields of Ch[...]*

Faulkner, William: *Light in August*

Forster, E. M.: *A Room with a View*

Franklin, Benjamin: *Poor Richard's Almanac, 1733-[...]*

Golding, William: *Lord of the Flies*

Heller, Joseph: *Catch-22*

Hobbes, Thomas: *Seven Philosophical Problems*

Hugo, Victor: *Les Miserables, Volume IV, Saint Deni[...]*

Huxley, Aldous: *Brave New World*

Irving, H. B.: *A Book of Remarkable Criminals*

Joyce, James: *Ulysses*

Kafka, Franz: *The Metamorphosis*

Lee, Harper: *To Kill a Mockingbird*

Livius, Titus: *The History of Rome, Vol. III*

Martin, Steve: *Cruel Shoes*

Miller, Arthur: *The Crucible*

Milton, John: *Paradise Lost*

Niehardt, John G.: *The Singing of the Frogs*

Orwell, George: *1984*

Plato: *The Republic of Plato*

Poe, Edgar Allan: *The Murders in the Rue Morgue*

Rose, Jim: *Freak Like Me*

Salinger, J.D.: *Catcher in the Rye*

Shakespeare, William: *Hamlet*

Shatner, William: *Star Trek Memories*

Shelley, Mary: *Frankenstein*

Sugimoto, Hanano Inagaki: *The Ivory Skull*

Thoreau, Henry David: *Walden, or Life in the Woods*

Twain, Mark, pseud. (Samuel Langhorne Clemens): In[...] Abroad

Wells, H. G.: *The Island of Doctor Moreau*

Fallout P-38 Secret Message Cannon

Need to get a secret message out there, and your radio-communicators just won't do the trick? Here's a way to get a message out fast, and use codes that leave the villains scratching their heads. Simply write your message, put it within the Secret Message Shells (sold separately), calibrate the visual target system, and fire away! Your message is launched with the super pinpoint accuracy that you want and need. Order now and get a free copy of "Professor Puzzler's Fun & Easy Guide to Secret Codes!"

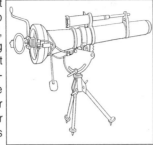

Secret Message Shells (N-Gage)

Need to send a lot of messages? You'll find these extra shells a supervalue. Sturdy and strong, made from high-impact postindustrial materials. Simple screw-top makes the shell "user-friendly!" A must!

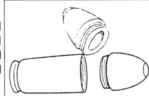

Pendecker Series 7 Pneumatic Grappling Hook with Full Body Harness and Power Winch

Rooftop distance getting you down? Say good-bye to pesky boomerangs. This pneumatic grappling hook will get you moving in no time! Specially designed grappling hook gets you a strong hold every time. Power Winch won't let you down, in either rain, sleet, or a hail of bullets! Multi-adjustable body harness gives a perfect fit to all superheroes and heroines, whether you are TinyMan or Mr. Massive... or even Sexy-Lass! 200 feet of Pendecker superhero gauge cable included.

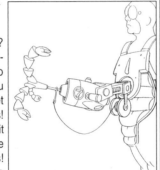

"My First" Junior Crime Lab Chemistry Set

Crime fighting and detective work will be a breeze with this kit. Analyze fingerprints, create antidotes, and amaze your friends. A true full-functioning crime headquarters cannot afford to be without this fabulous set of equipment. Comes with everything you need to set yourself on the exciting road of crime-busting chemistry in just minutes.

Mayor: And I'd like to thank The Tick, Arthur, and American Maid for coming through when The City needed them the most.

Tick: Thank you, Mayor Blank. We all enjoyed saving your life. Y'know, evil comes in many forms, whether it be a man-eating cow or Joseph Stalin, but you can't let the package hide the pudding! Evil is just plain bad! You don't cotton to it. You gotta smack it in the nose with the rolled-up newspaper of goodness! Bad dog! Bad dog! And you don't do it for money. No! You do it for love! You know, I've learned something this week– on justice and on friendship, there is no price. But there are established credit limits.

MIGHTY BLUE JUSTICE!

Announcer: And the East Coast was literally shaken by the return of Blow-Hole, the legendary long-distance leviathan, who ten years ago baffled the nation when he jumped out of the Pacific Ocean and ran straight across the country. One week later, Blow-Hole plunged into the icy waters of the Atlantic, disappearing without a comment. Is he planning a return trip? One thing is for certain, nobody knows.

YES, MY SLIMY FRIEND, ONCE AGAIN SLIME DOES NOT PAY! YOU CAN'T JUST COAT YOURSELF WITH ARTIFICIAL MUCOUS AND SLIP THROUGH THE LONG FINGERS OF THE LAW. IT'S WRONG AND IT'S GROSS.

PATROLLING WITHOUT A SIDEKICK— IT'S UNNATURAL!

WHAT'S THIS?! IT'S A LITTLE BOY'S FACE! OH, DON'T WORRY, LITTLE BOY, I'LL FREE YOU FROM THIS BLOCK OF WOOD!

Arthur's Casebook:

While Tick and I were out apprehending the villain The Red Herring, we were approached by a woman in a flying moth suit just like mine! Her name was Carmelita, and she said she had been looking all over the world... for ME! It turns out the inventor of my suit, J. J. Eureka Vatos, was her father. She had a notebook with more of her father's ingenious inventions, but the entire book was written in a secret code. The key to the code, her father had told her, was hidden in one of the moth suits, and it had to be mine! Carmelita was really nice. I like her a lot! I walked her home instead of going out on patrol, which I don't think The Tick liked too much. He went on patrol without me. Later Carmelita and I went out to dinner, and I had to skip "Hobby Night" with The Tick, which, again, made him kinda mad. He just doesn't understand! But that night, when we were out for dinner, we were attacked by a group of yodeling Swiss Industrial Spies, who (Carmelita told me) were after her father's book and the key to the code. The Swiss had these big multipurpose army knives. Even with the help of American Maid, Die Fledermaus, Sewer Urchin, and then even The Tick, the Swiss managed to get away with my pants and the book. I took one of the Swiss's big knives and with it managed to get everything back. As Carmelita and I gazed into each other's eyes, caught up in our victory, we were... swallowed by Blow-Hole! There, amazingly enough, we found Carmelita's father, J. J. Eureka Vatos, in the belly of the running whale! We used a chunk of wood that The Tick was carrying around to start a fire (which seemed to upset him a little), which caused Blow-Hole to sneeze us out.

DON'T EVER TRY TO SWIM AGAINST THE MIGHTY TIDE OF JUSTICE.

103

THE TICK'S STUFF

HOW TO MAKE A LITTLE WOODEN BOY:

1. FIND A PIECE OF WOOD. BUT NOT ANY PIECE OF WOOD WILL DO, NO! FIND A PIECE OF WOOD THAT ALREADY HAS A LITTLE WOODEN BOY TRAPPED INSIDE. YOUR JOB IS TO SET THAT LITTLE GUY FREE!
2. GET TOGETHER THESE ITEMS:

3. PUT YOUR LITTLE WOODEN BOY TOGETHER. HERE'S WHAT MY LITTLE WOODEN BOY LOOKED LIKE: REMEMBER TO HAVE A PARENT OR AN ADULT HELP YOU WITH THE NAILS AND STUFF, AND ALLOW TIME FOR THE PAINT TO DRY, OR IT COULD MAKE AN ICKY MESS, ALL OVER YOUR CLEAN SUPERHERO GLOVES!
4. NOW GET OUT THERE AND FIGHT! FIGHT FOR THE SIDE OF ALL THAT IS GOOD AND RIGHT!

Sally Vacuum: It's Blow-Hole 1995! This is Sally Vacuum reporting from the outskirts of The City. And you can just feel the "Blow-Hole Mania" out here, as hundreds of area residents gather to wish Blow-Hole well. Here he comes! Blow-Hole, is this cross-country run a form of protest for the endangered species of the Earth?

Blow-Hole: ...

Sally Vacuum: If you were a tree, what kind of tree would you be?

Blow-Hole: ...

Sally Vacuum: Blow-Hole! Do you have time for a few questions?

Blow-Hole: ...sigh...

Sally Vacuum: Where do you see yourself in ten years -

<TRANSMISSION LOST>

THE TICK'S STUFF

Arthur's Casebook:

The Tick was picked by the National Space Program to travel to the Moon and help repair the damage done earlier by Chairface Chippendale. But in a freak accident, while he

> SPACE, THE FINAL FRONTIER, THE GREAT BLACK BLANKET. MAN, A GUY CAN GET BORED OUT HERE. AH... SPACE HURTS.

was trying to fix the letter "C", the explosives went off early, blowing up The Tick. We all thought he was... DEAD! Everyone was pretty upset. The City put up a big statue of The Tick, and Mayor Blank gave me a nice cheese basket (which Die Fledermaus ate most of). It was all pretty depressing. I tried to be Die Fledermaus's sidekick, but... I don't know about that guy. All we really did was look through fashion magazines and pose on top of buildings. Then I tried to be The Human Bullet's sidekick, but that was just... frightening. I decided to "go solo," and while I was out after the Whirlin' Scottish Devil, The Tick flew in from space on a giant shoe! The Tick was back! But with The Tick came Omnipotus, a giant cosmic space being who wanted to eat the Earth. The Tick tried to stop Omnipotus by showing him all that is wonderful about the Earth, like bowling trophies and paint-by-numbers sets, which, I guess, was the best he could do at the time. It turns out, all Omnipotus really wanted was a friend. The Tick said he'd be his friend if he would spare our planet. He did, but took a giant bite out of the Moon on his departure. At least Tick was back.

> SO THE COSMIC CIRCUS MOVES ALONG, ITS TINIEST CLOWN GONE TO REJOIN IT ONCE AGAIN.

MIGHTY BLUE JUSTICE!

Brian Pinhead: The lunar lander has touched down successfully. We are about to witness history in the making. Very shortly the specially appointed team of astronauts will set out on an unprecedented mission to repair the damage done to the surface of the Moon last year, when the infamous crimelord Chairface Chippendale attempted to carve his name into it with the use of a powerful laser cannon during a birthday party gone bad. Chairface was thwarted in the middle of the act by The City's own superhero, The Tick, who was then chosen to be a part of this historic lunar repair mission, making him the first superhero to take part in an official space shot. The astronauts are now waiting for the go-ahead from National Space Program headquarters in Houston.

Ground Control: You are a go, lunar team.
Tick: This is one small step for The Tick, and one giant step for... say, a little bug. Or some guy who's been shrunk to the size of a penny.
Ground Control: You can talk to him direct by pressing this. Go ahead, Arthur.
Arthur: How's everything going with the mission so far? Tick, remember, the whole world is watching.
Tick: I'm watching you, too, world! Oh boy!

Brian Pinhead: The astronaut team is made up of expert scientists and construction workers from around the world. They will be working with extremely dangerous explosives. Absolute precision is necessary to guarantee their safety.

Astronaut 1: That's enough TNT to blow us all off this rock. I say let the indestructible guy do the dirty work.

Astronaut 2: Tick! Hey, Tick! Come here. Want to have some real fun? Here's the plan, superhero. Take this jetpack, fly down into those letters with the explosive charges.

Tick: Jetpack! Slick!

Astronaut 2: Uh huh. So you take the jetpack, and you fly down into that great big letter "C."

Tick: Into the belly of the Moon!

Astronaut 2: Okay, settle down. Now, this is your basic high explosive charge with a detonator switch. Now, when you get to the bottom of the channel, place the explosive pack on the side wall, climb back up here to a safe distance, and hit that detonator button. Piece of cake, buddy!

Tick: Hey! Where did everybody go?

Astronaut 2: Minimum safe distance, Tick. We'll all be here in the lander... monitoring your progress. Yeah, that's it. Break a leg, big guy!

Brian Pinhead: The Tick has just been briefed on the task before him. And we will return with live coverage of the mission. Meanwhile, in a related story, the National Space Program has just informed us that it has lost contact with the Quixote space probe launched over three years ago. All scientists know is that at the time it disappeared, the probe was, quote, "really, really far away."

Tick: Y'know, citizens of Earth, when I look back at that big beautiful blue ball we call "home," I can't help but get a little misty. I mean, what's our problem anyway? Why can't we all just join hands and...

Yank: Scree! Scree! Scree!

Ground Control: Uh, Tick, can we get a move on here?

Tick: Uh, right. Check. That's a big ten-forty. Roger and out.

Ground Control: It looks like he's ready.

Tick: And now, Space-Tick soars into history!

<EXPLOSION. TRANSMISSION BROKEN>

Arthur: Aaaaaaaaaahhhhhhhh!!!!!!!

Superhero/Astronomy News

In Memory of The Tick
The Tick Gives His Own Life to Save the Moon.

The entire world was saddened last week with the horrible news that The City's – if not the world's – greatest superhero, The Tick, lost his life trying to save the Moon. In what was an ambitious National Space Program mission to literally "erase" the letters "CHA" that were written on the Moon, The Tick lost his life in what was a freak explosion mishap.

Earlier this week, The City's mayor, the honorable Mayor Blank, presented a commemorative statue to the grieving citizens and The Tick's surviving sidekick, Arthur.

"And so citizens, we are gathered here today to pay tribute to the memory of one of The City's tallest, bluest, and best superheroes," Mayor Blank said in his speech to the crowd, which included some of The City's other notable superheroes. "Too soon The Tick was plucked from our midst and hurled screaming into the heavens. What a guy. And to commemorate his great sacrifice, the city council has commissioned this beautiful fiberglass-resin statue to stand forever in his honor." The crowd cheered with awe as the statue was revealed.

"Arthur, you may think that nothing can fill the void left in your life by The Tick's untimely departure from this world, but the city council has also commissioned for you this deluxe assortment of cheeses in this handcrafted wicker basket." Arthur seemed pleased by the presentation, but could not be reached for comment.

Our most patriotic superheroine, American Maid, was present, and said to us, "Fighting alongside The Tick was a pleasure, and an honor. He will be missed."

Die Fledermaus, also in attendance, commented on the statue, "The head is way too big!"

THE TICK'S STUFF

Die Fledermaus

Press release:

For immediate release.

Die Fledermaus, The City's most stylish hero, is pleased to announce his latest, greatest sidekick: Arthur. From this day on, villains should beware: the world's greatest super team, Die Fledermaus and Arthur, are now ready to keep The City safe!

"This is a good move for the little guy. Especially after his recent tragedy, with that whole Tick-killed-in-space bugaboo," Die Fledermaus said. "Arthur needs the guidance and support that only a sensitive nineties guy like me can give."

So look to the skies and feel safe, for Die Fledermaus and Arthur the Moth-Wonder are looking out for you!

Super Hero Not Dead.

One of The City's superheroes, The Tick, who was believed to have been killed in a failed NSP mission two months ago, has returned to The City very alive. Undisclosed reports say he was just floating around in space all that time.

YOU KNOW, ARTHUR, WHEN YOU SPEND TWO MONTHS RIDING AROUND ON A REALLY BIG MAN, YOU START TO LEARN A FEW THINGS ABOUT YOURSELF. YOU LEARN THAT IT IS A REALLY GREAT THING TO STAY ON EARTH AND LIVE IN A PLACE THAT HAS NO ARMS OR LEGS OF ITS OWN. AND MOST IMPORTANTLY, ARTHUR, YOU LEARN HOW TO CLOSE YOUR EYES AND TELL YOURSELF THAT THIS JUST ISN'T HAPPENING TO ME. SO, DID YOU MISS ME?

I HOPE YOU DIDN'T SKIP PART 4! IF SO, TURN TO PAGE 76!

108
HA

MIGHTY BLUE JUSTICE!

Brian Pinhead: This is Brian Pinhead, with the latest on this fast-breaking story. The former superheroes known as The Tick and Arthur have joined forces with the evil love goddess Venus and embarked on a terrifying crime spree. This security video from a midtown jewelry store clearly shows that the once beloved arachnid and his winged sidekick have stepped over the increasingly thin line between hero and villain.

WHEN EVIL SEES A TWIN-HEADED, ARTHUR POWERED, FLYING ENGINE OF JUSTICE BARRELING DOWN UPON IT, GREAT WILL BE ITS TREMBLING!

DON'T MAKE US BITE YOU IN HARD-TO-REACH PLACES!

TICK GOES BAD

TICK STEALS $20,000 EVENING GOWN... SIZE EXTRA LARGE

TICK IN LINGERIE HEIST OOO-LA-LA!

TICK WOMAN'S WEAR GAME SPREE CONTINUES – CITYWIDE MANHUNT FOR TICK

EATING KITTENS IS JUST PLAIN... PLAIN WRONG! AND NO ONE SHOULD DO IT EVER!

Arthur's Casebook:

The crime couple of Venus and Milo, who we had already defeated, shot us with a weird beam that caused our arms to fall off! Then they stole our arms and ran off. We tried to call for help to American Maid, but she wasn't in (she was out of the country toppling an unauthorized dictatorship), so we went to the Diner. There we found out that Venus and Milo had built robots and gave them our arms and were committing crimes all around The City. We were now fugitives even though the robots didn't look anything like us! We figured that based on Venus's crimes, she was putting together an outfit for the Enemy Awards. But only villains knew where the Enemy Awards were held, so we went to the Evil Eye Cafe to find out. To our surprise, we were greeted as fellow villains. But then they got a little suspicious of us, and challenged us to eat a kitten, which of course we couldn't do. We scared them off with Maneuver 14B, and so they told us where the awards were being held. The doorman at the awards was pretty strict about not getting in without an invitation, so we snuck in with the show's dancers, disguised as a giant lizard and a burning building. When Venus won the award for "Most Improved Villain of the Year," Tick and I took on her robots backstage. The Tick managed to talk his arms back to the side of good, and the robot beat himself up. Plunger Man (don't ask) was there to reattach our arms, and we were able to catch Venus and Milo, and clear our names.

VILLAIN LOVE GODDESS! YOU TOY WITH THE HEARTS OF MEN!

THE TICK'S STUFF

Merry Christmas

TO ALL OUR SUPER FRIENDS, MERRY CHRISTMAS TO ONE AND ALL! ARTHUR AND I INVITE YOU TO A FESTIVE TINSEL LADEN EVENING OF EGGNOG AND CAROLING! JOYEUX NOEL, TICK & ARTHUR

Arthur's Casebook:

With only two shopping days left, The Tick and I were out doing our last-minute Christmas shopping and getting things for our Christmas party. We ran into the police chasing down a rogue Santa, who had robbed a bank. The Tick got a little confused and couldn't understand why the police were chasing Santa. Anyway, we chased the Santa up on to a roof, and he fell off into a big electric sign. Tick was horrified. He felt responsible for "frying Santa" and that there would be no more Christmas. He was really depressed at the party, though we tried to tell him that the Santa wasn't real. When we all went out caroling, we were overrun by an army of Santas, led by the Santa we'd chased earlier. He called himself Multiple Santa. There were just too many Santas, and The Tick couldn't bring himself to hit Santa, or ANY Santa. He just stood there. We got stomped. The Tick still didn't know that Santa wasn't real; he just wouldn't accept it. Afterward, we went home, and found the apartment full of... elves! They said they were Santa's Little Secret Service! They brought in the real SANTA! Santa told us about how the Multiple Santas were evil and naughty, and how we had to save Christmas! We were on a mission from Santa! Santa told us that Multiple Santa was at the city dam, where he was going to launch his assault against Christmas. On our way there, we were hit by an avalanche of Santas. In the ensuing fight, we found that static electricity "shorted" the Santa clones out and made them disappear. We created a static chain reaction that made all the Santas disappear, and we were able to catch Multiple Santa... and save Christmas. Finally, I was able to actually see those dancing sugarplums (but I still didn't know exactly what sugarplums were).

LIKE A GREAT BLUE SALMON OF JUSTICE, THE MIGHTY TICK COURSES UPSTREAM TO THE VERY SPAWNING GROUND OF EVIL!

WAIT A MINUTE, YOU! I HEARD ABOUT PEOPLE LIKE YOU. ARE YOU SAYING YOU DON'T BELIEVE IN SANTA CLAUS?! AND YOU CALL YOURSELF SUPERHEROES?

To: The Tick
From: Die Fledermaus
Re: How to identify the real Santa

If Santa jumps up and kicks you in the stomach, it is probably NOT SANTA, you dink!
- DF

Brian Pinhead: Earlier today, the Santa clones cleaned out the Must-Go-Shopping Plaza, terrifying last-minute shoppers and destroying a very expensive News 17 camera. Of course, the camera can always be replaced.

THEIR ACHILLES' HEEL IS THE NOOGIE!

THE TICK'S STUFF

Arthur's Casebook:

While out on patrol, I literally ran into Renaissance inventor Leonardo Da Vinci. He flew right into me! He told us how he (and Mona Lisa) were caught in a time vortex, and captured by a villain calling himself The Mother of Invention. This Mother of Invention, with his time machine, also kidnapped Thomas Edison, Johann Gutenberg, George Washington Carver, Benjamin Franklin, and Wheel (inventor of the wheel). His plan was to blow up the Renaissance with a time bomb, and then go and invent all the inventions of the past 600 years himself, and take all the credit. Using bunk beds, Leonardo created a flying machine to escape, and that's how he found us. Hearing how horrible this Mother of Invention's plan was, we took Leonardo home so he could build another flying contraption. Tick volunteered my couch and bicycle so he could make a new flying machine. While he worked, we were attacked by Mongols who were after Da Vinci! I was able to scare them off with a kitchen blender. When we got to The Mother of Invention's hideout, we had to face off against not only Mongols but ninjas, knights, and a rampaging elephant. Just when things were looking bad, the other inventors saved the day with this big invention that had a battering ram, and fired peanuts and stamped letters. But we gave The Mother of Invention enough time to fire off his time bomb. Tick had me send him through time, after the bomb, and then returned triumphant. He had saved the day—and all of time!

I'M FLYING... I SWOOP... I SOAR... THE CITY LAPS AT MY HEELS LIKE A GRATEFUL PUPPY. I AM THE EAGLE KING OF ALL I SURVEY. I AM BECOME SHIVA, DESTROYER OF WORLDS!

THE CITY BUILDING COMMISSION

Dear Tick,

It has come to our attention that your daily superhero patrols are causing a substantial amount of structural damage to rooftops, chimneys, water towers, and windows of both civic and privately owned buildings in The City. The City can only budget a certain amount of tax money to repair the damage caused by our superheroes, and our figures show that 92% of civic funds allotted to damage repair is being taken up by damage you are directly responsible for.

While The City is proud of our extensive and diversified superhero community, we must ask you to conduct your patrols in a less careless and destructive manner. If you do not change your patrol habits, we will be forced to have you pay the bills for damage repair, and we may be forced to take up your city placement with the National Super Institute review board.

Yours truly,

Nathan Nettlebaum

Nathan Nettlebaum
City Building Commissioner
NN/nw

YOU KNOW... I'VE HEARD THE SMARTER YOU ARE, THE MORE WRINKLY YOUR BRAIN. AND YOU GUYS' BRAINS MUST BE THE WRINKLIEST! OH, SURE, ORDINARY JOES LIKE ME AND ARTHUR HERE, MAYBE OUR BRAINS ARE A LITTLE ON THE SMOOTH SIDE. BUT YOU DON'T HAVE TO BE A GENIUS TO KNOW THAT EVIL IS BAD! AND GOOD ISN'T!

MIGHTY BLUE JUSTICE!

CAVE WOMAN SUES FOR BACK ROYALTIES ON THE WHEEL!

She's loaded!

The LOBSTER FACTORY'S favorite customer, Wheel-cave woman and celebrated inventor of the wheel-says:

"Big red bugs! MMMM! They're delicious!"

MIDNIGHT BOMBER SEZ: "HE SAYS, 'YOU WANNA BE A SUPER VILLAIN, RIGHT?' AND I GO, 'YEAH, BABY! YEAH!'"

THE TICK'S STUFF

Arthur's Casebook:

While out trying to put an end to what the news was calling "The Mad Nanny Crisis," The Tick and I came across The Mad Nanny in a big robotic exoskeleton. We weren't able to stop her, and she destroyed the Diner and captured The Tick. Fortunately, because of the Fiend Finder Tracking Device, a piece of crime fighting junk Tick ordered, American Maid, Die Fledermaus, Sewer Urchin, and I were able to track The Tick to the suburbs. There we discovered a much larger and more sinister plot than a mere Mad Nanny. We found The Tick in the clutches of the evil Brainchild, who had not only turned The Tick into a two-headed bird who spoke high-school French, but was trying to sell him off to a collection of the world's most fiendish and notorious super villains: Chairface Chippendale, Professor Chromedome, The Idea Men, Pineapple Pokopo, and The Terror. Die Fledermaus and Sewer Urchin disguised themselves as villains, and went in to bid for The Tick. Meanwhile, American Maid and I planned to use The Idea Men's blimp to grab Brainchild's transforming device and rescue The Tick. Flying a blimp is harder than it looks, and things didn't really go as planned. But we still managed to get in, and I was able to turn The Tick back to normal... once I found the "NORMAL" button. We chased all the villains away, but Brainchild sicked a newer, meaner version of his robot dog Skippy on The Tick. The ensuing fight destroyed the house, right as Brainchild's parents came home. We were able to take young Brainchild to the proper authorities.

> MAD NANNY! IF YOU HARM A HAIR ON THIS GREASY SPOON'S HEAD, YOU'LL HAVE THE TICK TO ANSWER TO.

> YOU JUST TOASTED THE BEST BLT JOINT IN THE TRISTATE AREA; PREPARE TO PICK UP THE TAB!

> JE M'APPELLE LE TIC. J'AI UNE GRANDE PLUME ET DEUX TETES.

> YOU KNOW, THOUGH TODAY WAS THE WORST DAY OF MY LIFE, I LEARNED MANY THINGS. FIRST, THE WORLD LOOKS A LOT DIFFERENT WHEN YOU'RE SIX INCHES TALL AND COVERED IN FEATHERS. SECOND, TWO HEADS ARE DEFINITE-LY NOT BETTER THAN ONE. AND FINALLY, YOU CAN LAY AN EGG AND STILL FEEL LIKE A MAN.

MIGHTY BLUE JUSTICE!

Brian Pinhead: Day four of The Mad Nanny Crisis. Officials have identified the so-called "Mad Nanny" as fifty-four-year-old Miriam Brunch, an employee of the highly regarded Miss Muffin Baby-Sitting Agency. The City continues to be terrorized by this rampaging domestic, who only moments ago destroyed Earl McBain's Old Time Toy and Memorabilia Shop. Mr. McBain was heard to ask, quote, "What kind of nanny would do this?" unquote.

NEXT TIME THEY WON'T GET AWAY WHEN YOU USE
THE FIEND FINDER™ 9000 TRACKING DEVICE!

EASY-READ SCREEN POINTS YOU RIGHT TO THE BAD GUYS! TINY TRACER BUG STICKS TO MOST SURFACES AND FABRICS! JUSTICE _WILL_ BE SERVED.

BE THE ENVY OF ALL YOUR OTHER SUPERHERO BUDDIES WHEN **YOU** CATCH THE BADDEST BAD GUY **FIRST!** FIEND FINDER™ COMES WITH EVERYTHING THAT YOU NEED TO START TRACKING EVIL ALL OVER YOUR NEIGHBORHOOD, CITY, OR COUNTRY*! AA BATTERIES NOT INCLUDED. JUST $24.95 (+$7.50 SHIPPING AND HANDLING. ALLOW 6-8 WEEKS FOR DELIVERY.)!!!
*FIEND FINDER™'S RANGE WILL NOT FACILITATE CROSS COUNTRY TRACKING (THE TERM "COUNTRY" JUST USED FIGURATIVELY).
FIEND FINDER™ NOT TO BE USED NEAR PREGNANT WOMEN, THE ELDERLY, SMALL CHILDREN, OR THE DENTALLY SENSITIVE. DO NOT HOLD TRACKING BUG NEAR FACE. FIEND FINDER™ MAY CAUSE PREMATURE HAIR LOSS.

☐ Yes! Send me a Fiend Finder™ 9000. Included is my $24.95 + $7.50 s&h.
☐ I've included an extra $4.95 for RUSH DELIVERY!
Name_____
Address_____

A GOOD SUPERHERO SKILL IS THE ART OF DISGUISE!

THE TICK'S STUFF

Arthur's Casebook:

My hay fever is really bad... I don't feel like writing this, but I will, nonetheless...

While attending the Annual Flower Show, Tick, American Maid, and I saw the world's oldest flower, the 400-year bloom. The flower's guardian, Professor Ikebana, told us how she has to keep playing music to the flower to keep it from blooming "the bad way," and also of the terrible things that would happen if the bloom fell into the wrong hands. Suddenly rogue saw-flowers attacked us, and as The Tick and American Maid fought the saw-flowers, Professor Ikebana took me aside and told us how a villain with a flower for a head, the evil El Seed, was after the 400-year bloom. She gave me the flower to protect. On the way home the tape-recorded music for the bloom ran out, and the flower began to grow at an incredible rate! We calmed it down by having American Maid sing to it. Later, we found out that Professor Ikebana was kidnapped by El Seed, so Tick and American Maid went out to rescue her, and I stayed with the bloom to make sure the music didn't stop. But then I was attacked by a seven-foot-tall rose-creature. The next thing I knew, Tick was waking me up, and the bloom was gone! Using my hay fever to find El Seed, we were able to track him to the City Botanical Gardens, where El Seed had allowed the bloom to grow to hundreds of feet. If the bloom kept growing, the plant would destroy The City, so The Tick had to sing to it. While The Tick sang, he was attacked by El Seed's big rose-creature, Rosebud. But Tick was able to sing Rosebud into submission, as well. El Seed finally showed up, and shot seeds down The Tick's throat. As corn and trees grew out of Tick's mouth, I had to sing to the growing bloom. It worked! The bloom returned to its small size, and I put on quite a show!

> BLOOM, LITTLE LEAFLING, MAKE GOOD YOUR HOLD UPON THE WORLD.

> VILE VINE, NOW MAYBE YOU'LL THINK TWICE BEFORE YOU EAT ANOTHER HUMAN BEING.

> WELL, IT JUST GOES TO SHOW, MOTHER NATURE HAS A LOAD OF TRICKS UP HER GREEN SLEEVES. AND TONIGHT SHE REALLY PUT HER FOOT DOWN. YES, HERE'S YOUR LITTLE FLOWER, PROFESSOR, AND NEXT TIME IT BLOOMS, MAY IT BLOOM IN THE GOOD WAY!

MIGHTY BLUE JUSTICE!

AMERICAN MAID INVITES YOU TO THE

annual Flower Show!

COME SEE THE 400-YEAR BLOOM ON ITS FABULOUS AMERICAN TOUR. NEW YORK! HOBOKEN! LOS ANGELES! AND NOW THE CITY!

Incredible Growing Flower Ravages City!

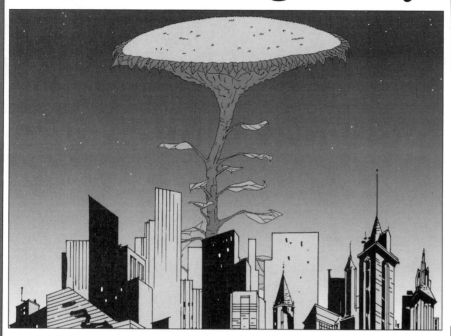

Announcer: We interrupt tonight's program for a special news bulletin. Terror erupted today at the annual civic flower show when Professor Akito Ikebana, noted botanist, was kidnapped. Ikebana was on a national tour exhibiting the very rare 400-year bloom, which also mysteriously disappeared. Authorities suspect foul play.

Not since the terrible rampage of Dinosaur Neil has The City been swept up in so much terror and destruction.

The 400-year bloom, which was on display at the Annual Flower Show, was stolen earlier in the day by supercriminal El Seed. The bloom's guardian, noted botanist Professor Akito Ikebana, was also kidnapped by El Seed. She had learned of his plan to allow the bloom to grow, and to control it to destroy humanity. Professor Ikebana was rescued from El Seed's leafy grasp by popular superheroes The Tick and American Maid.

Professor Ikebana told reporters of what could happen if the flower had a "bad blooming." "Eight hundred years ago we had a bad blooming. Practically wiped out the entire Mistermoto Dynasty."

The threat of the so-called "bad bloom" was nipped in the bud by The Tick and his winged sidekick Arthur. Other superheroes, American Maid and The Human Bullet, while claiming to have been helping in the fight against the bloom, were inexplicably found several miles away in nearby Deertown.

MIDNIGHT BOMBER SEZ: "AND I GO, 'YEAH, BABY, 'CAUSE I'M THE EVIL-MID-NIGHT-BOMBER-WHAT-BOMBS-AT-MIDNIGHT!'"

THE TICK'S STUFF

Arthur's Casebook:

We had Die Fledermaus meet us at Furniture-O-Rama to help us pick out some new furniture that was big (for The Tick) and cheap (for me). To our surprise, we found a lot of furniture that started walking around... and then attacking us! The furniture was being commanded by The Ottoman, a villainess who seemed to be quite taken by Die Fledermaus. And he seemed to like her, too. We figured that The Ottoman would next hit at Ivan the Furniture Czar's Furniture Warehouse, to put together her furniture army. We found her there, all right, and faced off against her furniture army again. We found out that she also had command of the World's Most Comfortable Chair, and its horrible comfort trapped The Tick. She escaped once again, but we recovered the chair. Later, we spotted Die Fledermaus on a flying carpet, having a candlelit dinner with The Ottoman. Tick, American Maid, and I managed to get up to the carpet to stop The Ottoman, but in the ensuing fight, we were hit by an airplane (something I'd never imagined would happen to me). I managed to catch American Maid, but Tick fell 4,000 feet and was then hit by a subway train. He was (understandably) a little loopy. He thought he was now a duchess, or something. The Ottoman found us back at my apartment, and we were surrounded by angry furniture. We lured her up to the roof and were able to trap her in the World's Most Comfortable Chair. The move not only rehabilitated The Ottoman, but bumped Tick on the head, so he was back to normal. Relatively speaking.

YEAH, I AGREE, FALLING IN LOVE WITH A SUPER VILLAIN IS TROUBLE WITH A CAPITAL TROUB!

OTTOMAN, THERE'LL BE NO JUSTICE OF THE PEACE FOR YOU; JUST A BIG PIECE OF JUSTICE!

OH, LOOK, ARTHUR, IT'S A COMPLETELY REHABILITATED VILLAIN. SHE'S COMFORTABLE WITH HERSELF. COMFORT, COMMITMENT, MARRIAGE, WHAT DO THESE THINGS HAVE IN COMMON? THE LETTER C EXCEPT FOR MARRIAGE, AND IF PEOPLE GET ALL BRITISH WHENEVER THEY GET KNOCKED ON THE HEAD, WHAT DO BRITISH PEOPLE GET? I KNOW... COMATOSE! ANOTHER "C."

MIGHTY BLUE JUSTICE!

Things To Do and See in The City!

New this week to The City, at the Museum of Industrial Design, come and see the WORLD'S MOST COMFORTABLE CHAIR!

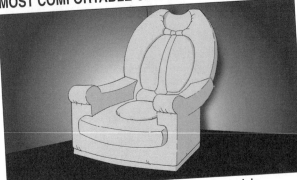

The World's Most Comfortable Chair was invented on June 14, 1953. The original test subject liked the chair so much, he sat in it until September 20, 1976; a shocking 23 years! Now the chair can be seen and marveled at in The City's fabulous Museum of Industrial Design.

Brian Pinhead: Although The Ottoman has amassed an army of furniture formidable enough to overpower The City's defenses, she appears to have diverted her energies to the pursuit of a single man, Die Fledermaus—one of The City's lesser heroes. We'll have more as the story develops.

TRANSCRIPT TAKEN FROM THE TELEVISION PROGRAM **HEROES:**

"YEAH, THE FIRST PATROL IS USUALLY PRETTY QUIET. YOUR AVERAGE VILLAIN PREFERS THE COVER OF NIGHT. YOU GET THE OCCASIONAL EVIL MORNING PERSON BUT RARELY BEFORE SEVEN. I DON'T KNOW WHY THAT IS. BY SEVEN-THIRTY, EIGHT O'CLOCK, EVIL IS WIDE-AWAKE. BUT WE'RE EVEN WIDER! WE'VE BEEN UP SINCE SIX-THIRTY! HELLO, TV LAND! I LOVE THIS SHOW! I WATCH THIS EVERY WEEK."

"I'M SURE MILLIONS OF VIEWERS OUT THERE ARE JUST WONDERING WHAT IT'S LIKE TO WEAR THE TIGHTS OF JUSTICE. WELL, IT'S TINGLY AND IT'S UNCOMFORTABLE, BUT IT GETS THE JOB DONE AND, OH, THE JOB OF IT!"

"OH, WHOA! KEEN! TICK CAM!"

"AFTER YEARS OF SUPERHERO TRAINING, YOU START TO NOTICE THAT A LOT OF THESE VILLAINS KINDA HAVE A MOTIF GOING. IN FACT, I BET MY BOTTOM DOLLAR THAT THE FOUR-STORY-TALL LIGHTBULB THERE HAS GOT SOMETHING TO DO WITH THE DEADLY BULB. PLUS, THAT'S ARTHUR."

"THIS IS WHAT WE HEROES CALL THE DENOUEMENT; THAT'S FRENCH FOR WHEN WE FINISH OFF THE SUPER VILLAINS."

"I'M A BLAZING FURNACE OF LIGHT ETCHED INTO THE FIRMAMENT. I GOT ME A CELESTIAL BODY NOW."

"OOH, HOTTER, BRIGHTER, I'M A FIERY NEW SUN...."

"HUH? THE UNIVERSE IS OVER AND MY SOLAR LIFE HAD JUST BEGUN."

"OH, LOOK, A LITTLE LUMPY WHITE PLANET. OH, IT'S A CHATTY MISSHAPEN THING DEVOID OF LIFE. I WILL BREATH MY WARMTH UPON IT."

"WELL, FOLKS, THERE YOU HAVE IT. A DAY IN THE LIFE OF A SUPERHERO AND HIS SIDEKICK. IT'S A VERY LONG DAY, THE TIGHTS ARE UNCOMFORTABLE; I THINK WE COVERED THAT BEFORE. MAP LIGHT, CONVENIENT AND ESSENTIAL. A LOT OF WORKING OF VILLAIN MOTIFS. CRIME HAS A BOSSA NOVA BEAT. LEAP BEFORE YOU LOOK. REMEMBER DENOUE-MENT. OTHER FRENCH WORDS: INCONVE-NIENT, NONESSENTIAL... OH... I COULD GO ON AND ON...BUT TIME'S A-WASTING AND EVIL'S OUT THERE MAKING HANDCRAFTED MISCHIEF FOR THE SWAP MEET OF VIL-LAINY. AND YOU CAN'T STRIKE A GOOD DEAL WITH EVIL. NO MATTER HOW MUCH YOU HAGGLE! WE DON'T NEED TO LOOK FOR A BARGAIN; GOODNESS IS CHEAP BECAUSE IT'S FREE, AND FREE IS AS CHEAP AS IT GETS. CUT! WHAT WAS THAT PIG ABOUT?"

Arthur's Casebook

While on our patrol of The City, The Tick and I came across a new villain, The Deadly Bulb, floating in a lightbulb balloon, and causing the power to go out in the area. The Tick man-aged to deflate the bal-loon, but The Deadly Bulb and his henchmen, Watt and Socket, got away by blind-ing The Tick. We also had the camera crew from the TV show *Heroes* with us, and The Tick, who was kind of blinded and confused, sort of attacked the cameraman. Back at the diner, the guys from *Heroes* gave The Tick his own camera to kind of, I guess, distract him. But then, the next thing we knew, The Deadly Bulb attacked the Diner, and kidnapped me and the camera crew. The Deadly Bulb dan-gled me around a giant lightbulb, and then after he captured The Tick, he used him as a filament for the giant bulb in an attempt to fry both me and The Tick. Fortunately, American Maid showed up, defeated The Deadly Bulb, and cut the power to the giant bulb. The Deadly Bulb gave up on his lightbulb villain motif and became Pigleg—probably because he had a pig for a leg... which is pretty weird.

119

THE TICK'S STUFF

Deertown T.V. Listings - Saturday the 18th
FIGHT THE GOOD FIGHT! CLOSE-UP AND REAL!
SATURDAY AT 8!
HEROES
THIS WEEK: THE CITY'S TICK, AND A VILLAIN WITH A PIG FOR A LEG.
37
HERE'S A LITTLE TIP. LEAP BEFORE YOU LOOK!
ARTHUR! HONK IF YOU LOVE JUSTICE!
DEADLY BULB, I'M ABOUT TO WRITE YOU A REALITY CHECK! OR WOULD YOU PREFER THE COLD HARD CASH OF TRUTH?
ROOF-PIG! MOST UNEXPECTED.
SO WARM, SO BRIGHT, ITCHY ALL OVER. I'M TWINKLING... I'M TWINKLING.
HAPPY ME, I'M THE BIGGEST, BRIGHTEST BALL OF GAS IN THE COSMOS.
MIGHTY BLUE JUSTICE!

ANT MENACE!

After ant theft spree, City officials decide what to do.
Anthill grows at alarming rate!

> **AHA! SO, BAD LADY, FATE HAS PUT A DEAD END TO YOUR ANARCHY DABBLING!**

As the mysterious ants gather up glass from all over The City, Mayor Blank and City officials wonder what they can do. While it is known that the ants are responsible for the glass theft, what to do with the ants is still unknown.

"Technically, we are not dealing with thieves," Mayor Blank told reporters, "We are dealing with ants, and therefore they are not subject to the criminal justice system. I feel this is a matter for the Department of Sanitation to deal with."

Police Chief Doodlehead has other solutions, as he wants the police to apprehend the ants. "We've been working on tiny handcuffs for just such a problem."

Outside sources are also offering solutions to the ant crisis. Noted scientist Herr Professor has proposed building a giant bar of nougat, to be the biggest candy bar ever constructed, outside The City to lure the ants away. "Ants are nuts for nougat!" Herr Professor told us. The nougat would be tainted with nitroglycerine to poison, or possibly blow up, the ants. Herr Professor was last heard from a year ago when he built giant pants to help out in the Dinosaur Neil crisis.

Inside sources in City Hall told us that other plans of action include consulting the National Guard, and possibly getting a superhero, such as The Tick, involved in handling the ant crisis.

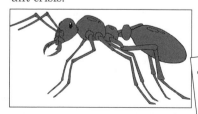

Ants! Not our little friends anymore.

> **SANITY! YOU'RE A MADMAN!**

Arthur's Casebook:

Tick and I investigated a heist at Shiny Pretty Things jewelry store, where all that was stolen was the glass from the window. We found a mysterious woman making her getaway with the window, and Tick went off after her. I couldn't keep up, so I don't know what happened, but The Tick just ran away running and screaming! The next thing I knew, The Tick checked himself into Captain Sanity's Superhero Sanatorium. It seems these women who were stealing glass all around The City were in fact ants, and The Tick is afraid of ants. American Maid and I went and followed these intelligent ants to find they already had a giant anthill that was hundreds of feet tall. We met up at the anthill with Die Fledermaus, Sewer Urchin, and Fish Boy. Getting into the ant hill posing as exterminators, we found out that the ants were melting down all the glass, and were planning to make a giant magnifying glass. Then ants caught us and put us in a giant ant-farm... or rather, a PEOPLE-FARM! Betty, the ant queen, announced that the ants were no longer content with their treatment by the human world and turned the magnifying glass upon The City. Suddenly, The Tick showed up! Putting The City's safety ahead of his phobias, he fought the ants and caught the ant queen.

> **HEY! YOU IN THE PUMPS! I SAY TO YOU, "STOP BEING BAD!"**

> **AND THAT'S JUST IT, DOC- MY MIND HAS ALWAYS BEEN MY ACHILLES' HEEL!**

THE TICK'S STUFF

YOU KNOW, COME TO THINK OF IT, I'M NOT AFRAID OF ANTS. I NEVER WAS. IT'S JUST WHEN THEY ALL COME RUNNING OUT OF A LADY'S PANTS LIKE THAT... YECH... CREEPY. AND ISN'T SANITY REALLY JUST A ONE TRICK PONY ANYWAY? I MEAN ALL YOU GET IS ONE TRICK, RATIONAL THINKING, BUT WHEN YOU'RE GOOD AND CRAZY, OOOH, OOOH, OOOH, THE SKY IS THE LIMIT!

AHA, YES, I SEE...A CHOREOGRAPHIC CONUNDRUM. WHOA, WELL THAT WAS A LITTLE DANCEY. YOU KNOW WHY SUPER VILLAINS ARE SO UNHAPPY, ARTHUR? THEY DON'T TREASURE THE LITTLE THINGS.

Announcer: This is not a test. Authorities have issued a citywide alert. Please stay tuned to this station for emergency evacuation instructions.

Brian Pinhead: LEAVE THE CITY!!!

MIGHTY BLUE JUSTICE!

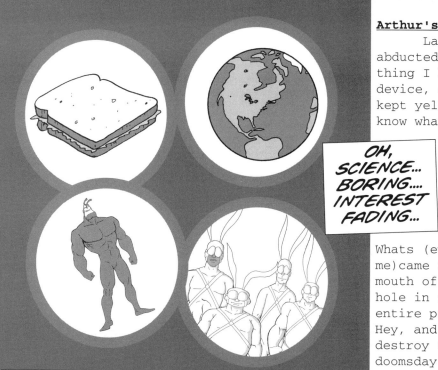

Last night, The Tick and I were abducted by space aliens. The next thing I knew, I was strapped to this device, and this big space alien just kept yelling "Hey" at me. I didn't know what he wanted. Then he tried to erase my mind, and I'm not sure what happened next, but they returned me to The Tick, who seemed to be getting along with the aliens a lot better than I had. It seems that the aliens, called the Whats (evil aliens who look like me) came to get us to go into the mouth of a black hole in front of the entire population of Hey, and steal or destroy their doomsday device. We got to the Hey ship just as the Hey leader threw the doomsday bomb into the black hole. The Tick was able to fight the laws of physics and reach into the black hole and pull the bomb out. But then the Heys turned their most horrible weapon on us, the Infinity Ball (which looked a lot like an 8-ball), but The Tick took care of it with one little punch. The Heys worshiped The Tick as a god, and that's how we saved the universe!

OH, SCIENCE... BORING.... INTEREST FADING...

HEY, WE'VE GOT THESE ON EARTH. WE KNOCK THEM INTO LITTLE POCKETS WITH STICKS. UH-HUH, AND WE GOT HIGHER NUMBERS, TOO.

GOT TO PULL MYSELF TOGETHER... MUST DEFY LAWS OF PHYSICS.

Did you ever think of the end of the universe? No? Well, let's give it a thought, shall we?

Here's your favorite sandwich, a BLT. It's delicious. And now... it's gone!

Here's your favorite planet, the Earth. It's where you keep all your stuff. And now... it's gone!

And here you are. You're just minding your own business. And now... you're gone!

To understand the end, let's go back to the beginning: the Big Bang. According to our theory, the Big Bang was the cosmic event in which all space, time, matter, and energy was formed.

Nothing. The Big Nothing. That's what the Heys want. They worship Nothing. Just listen to this Hey propaganda.

"Hey!" —Nothing lasts forever.

"Hey!" —Nothing is worth fighting for.

"Hey!" —Yes, we have no bananas.

Come to fabulous RENO, NEVADA,
And see
A great artist! A great mammal!

MR. SMARTY-PANTS

The smartest dolphin in the world!

OKAY, JACK, THIS LITTLE MINNOW HAS BEEN PLAYING HOOKY. ANY IDEA WHERE IT GOES TO SCHOOL?

AND MY MIDDLE NAME USED TO BE HELPING PEOPLE, THE "HELPING PEOPLE" TICK.

See Mr. Smarty-Pants as: He jumps through hoops!
He writes haiku! He wears pants!
See just how smart Mr. Smarty-Pants is!
Four shows nightly! Kids under 12 see Mr. Smarty-Pants free!

Below I dream of fish,
above me wretched
siblings prance in sequins.

Arthur's Casebook:

The Tick and I were called to Reno, Nevada, by Soren and Fredrica, to investigate the kidnapping of their famous performing dolphin, Mr. Smarty-Pants (he could write haiku!). The Tick (literally) stumbled upon a clue, a fish, that could lead us to Mr. Smarty-Pants. We went to Two-Eyed Jack's UFO Landing Strip and Quality Fish Market. Two-Eyed Jack told us the people who ordered the fish were coming back for more, so we planned to hide in a barrel of fish and let the crooks take us to their hideout. But Tick wandered off into a casino, and only Soren and Fred were taken away. Now we had to find them, too! I had to yell at The Tick because he was caught up in "Gambling Fever." Two-Eyed Jack told us where to find Mr. Smarty-Pants, Soren, and Fred, and loaned us his motorcycle to get to them (we looked pretty cool riding his "hog"!). We found an aquarium where Soren and Fred were being dangled in a pair of pants. Tick rescued them before the pants were set on fire. We found out that the whole plan was Mr. Smarty-Pants's. But he wasn't Mr. Smarty-Pants anymore; he now called himself The Fin, and told us of how he was going to bury Reno in fish with his Fish Magnet, which didn't really worry us until he turned the fish magnet on, and it worked. It was raining fish. The Tick distracted The Fin in a breath-holding competition, while I went to reverse the polarity on the Fish Magnet. The Tick won! Later on, the courts ordered that Soren and Fred were The Fin/Mr. Smarty-Pants's rightful guardians, and he had to perform for them, and they changed the act to "Mr. Smarty-Pants, the World's Most Angry Talking Dolphin."

AND SO, ARTHUR, WE LEARNED THAT GAMBLING IS BAD AND YET IN A CERTAIN SENSE ISN'T LIFE ITSELF A GAMBLE? YOU CAN NEVER REALLY BE SURE OF ANYTHING. LIKE WHO WOULD HAVE THOUGHT THAT DOLPHINS COULD GO BAD AND THAT FISH WERE MAGNETIC. NOT ME, NO SIR, NOT ME.

THE TICK'S STUFF

Arthur's Casebook:

While on our way home from visiting Captain Decency and the Decency Squad at Commander Goodbye's Superhero Retirement Home, we came across The Terror breaking The Human Ton and Handy out of prison. With him was a guy who was snooping around at the retirement home, who kept asking about something called the Desirovac. The Desirovac was a device that gave you anything you wished for. The Terror had used it in the forties; but it somehow got away from him, and the Decency Squad hid it. We figured The Terror was going after the Desirovac. We found the vault where it was hidden, but The Terror had already gotten his hands on it. He wished The Tick's antennae off his head, which caused The Tick to completely lose his balance. Apparently, that's what antennae do. With The Tick unable to even stand up, the Decency Squad actually took on The Human Ton, while The Terror fought with his son (the guy from the retirement home). I used the Desirovac to get Tick's antennae back, and he knocked the Human Ton out before he could step on The Living Doll. It seemed that the Decency Squad were actually going to put The Terror behind bars once and for all. And Tick and I stayed behind to destroy the Desirovac, so it could never be used for evil again.

> ARTHUR, YOU HAVE NO HISTORICAL PERSPECTIVE. SCIENCE IN THOSE DAYS WORKED IN BROAD STROKES. THEY GOT RIGHT TO THE POINT. NOWADAYS, IT'S ALL JUST MOLECULE, MOLECULE, MOLECULE. NOTHING EVER HAPPENS BIG.

> SO ONCE AGAIN, WE FIND THAT THE EVIL OF THE PAST SEEPS INTO THE PRESENT LIKE SALAD DRESSING THROUGH CHEAP WAX PAPER, MIXING MEMORY AND DESIRE.

MIGHTY BLUE JUSTICE!

The Terror Returns!
The Human Ton and Handy Escape from Jail!

Last night, The Terror showed up at the City Prison in his Spider-Mobile-Home to break arch criminal, and his former partner, The Human Ton, out of jail. The Human Ton's partner, Handy, believed to be merely a very nasty hand puppet, also escaped.

While The Terror's plans for The Human Ton are unknown, police and experts believe it can't be for good.

CASE CLOSED! Captain Decency and the Decency Squad Catch Their Man AFTER 50 YEARS!

Last night, to the surprise of everyone, retired superheroes Captain Decency and the Decency Squad showed up unexpectedly with their arch nemesis, The Terror! The group was also accompanied by The Terror's son, who supported turning his villainous father in.

The Terror, who just last night broke another notable super villain, The Human Ton, out of jail, was involved in a scheme to steal a device known as the Desirovac, which he used for the purpose of evil fifty years ago. The Desirovac was long thought to have been destroyed.

The Decency Squad, who now live at Commander Good-bye's Superhero Retirement Home, stopped fighting crime in the late 1950s. That is until last night! When a representative from Commander Good-bye's was asked if he knew about the Decency Squad's latest exploits, he said, "I thought they were in their rooms."

To The Tick,
Keep on fighting, son! You make us proud!

V·E

The Viswab Eye

Sufrajet

Captain Decency

The Living Doll

MIDNIGHT
BOMBER SEZ:
"AND SO HE SAYS TO ME, 'YOU GOT
LEGS BABY! YOU'RE EVERYWHERE!
YOU'RE ALL OVER THE PLACE!!'"

THE TICK'S STUFF

Arthur's Casebook:

This morning, when The Tick got up, he had a mustache! He was quite excited. I thought it was weird, because I had never even seen him shave. He walked around all day gloating, and having all the other superheroes tell him how good he looked. I, on the other hand, had better things to worry about. My sister, Dot, called to tell me that she and Dinosaur Neil were getting married! I had to throw an engagement party. The Tick was now talking to his mustache. He did it all night, too. I don't understand him sometimes. Now The Tick tells me his mustache moves, and writes him letters. I can't think about these things! Suddenly, at Dot and Neil's party, government agents showed up to fight The Tick's mustache. But the mustache wouldn't let itself be shaved. It kept leaping from upper lip to upper lip. Finally, the rogue mustache escaped, dragging Sewer Urchin with it. We found out the agents were from a team called SHAVE. Their leader, Special Agent Jim Rave, had been hunting the mustache all over the world for twenty years. We found the mustache and Sewer Urchin at the Dewey Bridge. We also found out that Project SHAVE lost its government funding in 1986, and that Jim Rave was just a nut. But he still wanted to destroy the mustache, and Sewer Urchin. Also at the bridge was a mysterious man known as the Russian Beard. This is the beard that the mustache wanted to meet, and they went off to live happily ever after.

> ARTHUR! MY MUSTACHE IS TOUCHING MY BRAIN!

> RUGGED. SELF-ASSURED. ADULT. THESE ARE THE WORDS THAT DESCRIBE THE MAN WHO WEARS A MUSTACHE. YES, IT SAYS TO THE WORLD, "I'M A MAN OF ACTION!" AH, BUT ACTION TEMPERED WITH MATURITY. LIKE A FIREMAN... OR SOMEBODY'S DAD! Y'KNOW, MOST OF YOUR WORLD LEADERS HAVE MUSTACHES!

> YOU CAN'T BLOW UP STINKY! HE'S NOT EVEN MOVING!

> SO THE MUSTACHE WAS IN LOVE. OH, THAT'S COOL. LOVE IS COOL. THAT MUSTACHE IS COOL. BUT IT DIDN'T MAKE ME COOL. IT MADE SEWER URCHIN SWING TEN MILES BY HIS UPPER LIP. AND LOOK AT JIM RAVE. HE SHOULD HAVE BEEN COOL. HE HAD A COOL EYE PATCH, COOL RV, COOL GADGETS, AND HE TRAVELED THE WORLD WITH THREE VIVACIOUS, EXCITING, TALENTED BEAUTICIANS. THAT'S COOL! BUT HE WASN'T COOL. YOU KNOW, ARTHUR, I MAY HAVE LOST MY MUSTACHE, BUT I'VE GAINED... I HAVEN'T GAINED A THING.

MY MUSTACHE WANTED THIS PAGE... BUT WHY???

FOUND IN SEWER One fragrant avenging bachelor. Please send photo.

YEAH, BABY, YEAH Explosive, dynamic go-getter seeks new mommy.

NOCTURNAL MAUS SEEKS KITTY CAT Toy with me.

HONEY-LOVING BEE TWINS Tired of the same old drones.

RB seeks mustache for serious relationship tomorrow night on the Dewey Bridge. - R.B.

IGNORE THE PIG Rehabilitated villain seeks pen pal for friendship, love, and conjugal visits.

BROWN SUGAR Our eyes met on the crosstown bus. I was the tall brunette in the red, white, and blue.

I HAVE A BABOON HEART and it's full of blood: SWM, smoker.

YOU CAUGHT MY EYE. Please give it back to me.

MIGHTY BLUE JUSTICE!

MUSTACHE!

GOT THAT FEELIN!
(OH YEAH!)
MUSTACHE FEELIN! IN MY SOUL.
GOT THAT FEELIN!
(COOL!)
FROM MY LIP DOWN TO MY TOES.
MUSTACHE!
HE AIN'T NOBODY'S FOOL.
(HO HO HA HA HA!)
HE GOT HIMSELF SOME COOL.
(UPPER LIP, SLICK AND HIP.
POINTY ON THE ENDS!)
MAKIN' A NEW SET OF FRIENDS.
(HA!)
GOT THAT FEELIN!
(LOOKIN! GOOD!)
MUSTACHE FEELIN!
OH, THAT MUSTACHE
KIND OF FEELIN'!!

THIS CHANGES EVERYTHING. I FEEL... DIFFERENT. BETTER. A NEW SENSATION IS SPREADING OUT FROM MY UPPER LIP TO EVERY OTHER PART OF MY BODY. IT'S A FEELING THAT I JUST CAN'T QUITE DESCRIBE. IT'S A SAVVY KIND OF FEELING. A SUAVEY KIND OF FEELING. KIND OF A... KIND OF A MUSTACHE FEELIN'!

THE TICK'S STUFF

Arthur's Casebook:

It was Dot and Dinosaur Neil's wedding and Tick was Neil's best man. I was really hoping everything would go all right. But suddenly a wreath of flowers turned into a monster and attacked Die Fledermaus. Then the wedding cake started to explode, and Tick had to eat it. This seemed to be the work of El Seed and The Breadmaster. Then during the ceremony, Neil turned giant again and ran off to destroy The City. It seems he had given The Tick instructions on what to do if this happened, but we needed a submarine and 1,400 pounds of pungent raw meat—items that Sewer Urchin actually had. Following Neil's instructions, we covered the sub with the meat, which proved tempting to Dinosaur Neil. Tick, Dot, and I got in, and allowed Neil to swallow us. We navigated our way to the base of Neil's brain, looking for swollen dinosaur DNA. When we got there, we found Indigestible Man, who had electrodes hooked up to

> MAN! TODAY IS SO LOOPY!

Neil's brain. Tick took care of Indigestible Man, and I took care of the swollen DNA strand. It worked, and Neil started to shrink, but we had to get out! We headed for his sinuses and were able to have him sneeze us out. We found out that Chairface had manipulated Neil's medicine, and was trying to control Dinosaur Neil to carry out his own destructive bidding. After Neil recovered, the wedding went off without a hitch.

> WHOA-OH! SURPRISE HUG FROM MR. FREAKY-BIG!

> THAW OUT THOSE COLD FEET! LET'S TALK THIS OVER!

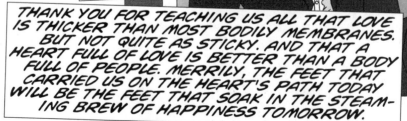

> THANK YOU FOR TEACHING US ALL THAT LOVE IS THICKER THAN MOST BODILY MEMBRANES. BUT NOT QUITE AS STICKY. AND THAT A HEART FULL OF LOVE IS BETTER THAN A BODY FULL OF PEOPLE. MERRILY, THE FEET THAT CARRIED US ON THE HEART'S PATH TODAY WILL BE THE FEET THAT SOAK IN THE STEAMING BREW OF HAPPINESS TOMORROW.

130

MIGHTY BLUE JUSTICE!

Brian Pinhead: That was the scene almost a year ago today, when Dinosaur Neil, noted paleontologist and curator of Dinosaur Grotto, accidentally consumed one of his own experiments and quote, "went Jurassic," unquote. But now instead of prehistoric fury and untold municipal destruction, it's wedding bells for Neil, as he plans to marry the sister of the sidekick of the superhero responsible for ending the errant fossil-finder's rampage last year and restoring him back to normal, The Tick.

Brian Pinhead: This is Brian Pinhead with a special report. It's Dinosaur Neil déjà vu. Evacuation of The City is under way, as Neil, who as you can see is bigger than ever, once again releases his "inner reptile."

DINOSAUR GROTTO

To whom it may concern,

If you're reading this, then I'm probably destroying The City. After careful research, I have concluded that my dinosaur DNA has been mutating. I'm afraid that if I grow again, then my medication will cease having an effect.

To help me get back to normal, I deduce that you will have to acquire a small submarine and 1,400 lbs. of pungent raw meat. Cover the sub with the raw meat and have a team of qualified people get in. The odor of the meat will certainly attract me. Allow me to swallow the sub. When inside me, follow the map included in this envelope. Precise instructions are on the map.

I'm sorry that you may have to perform this task, but it may be the only hope for myself, my loved ones, and The City.

Good Luck and Thank You Again,

Dinosaur Neil

Arthur's Casebook:

As strange as it may seem, I was abducted by Aztecs. Aztecs—not space aliens (I've already been abducted by space aliens...). I was out seeing a movie with Carmelita, and The Tick showed up. I thought he was just trying to bug me, telling me he followed ancient Aztecs in. But he was right, and when I went to get popcorn, they grabbed me. It seems these Aztec guys thought I was Carmelita, and they grabbed me by accident. The Aztec leader got really angry when he found out I was on a date with Carmelita, and they put me in their dungeon. They made me wear this funny dresslike costume, then they told me that they were preparing me for marriage. They were going to have me marry this weird dog thing. Then they catapulted me into a volcano, and Carmelita was actually there to catch me! We ended up surrounded by the Aztecs... but Carmelita knew them. It seems that all these Aztecs were Carmelita's old grade school baseball team, the Deertown Aztecs. I was put into another dungeon with a man who was the Aztec's baseball coach. It seems that the team's plane crashed in Mexico while on its way to the International Championship Game. With a book that they had about Aztecs, the kids decided to live in the ruins and act like Aztecs. The Tick was thrown into the dungeon, too, but at least he had the power to get us out. When we escaped the dungeon, we found Carmelita had taken care of Wally Head, the Aztec leader, and gotten my wings back. We all went back to The City and turned the boys over to the police. Tick decided to keep the dog thing I was supposed to marry. He calls it Speak, because "that's what he does." Sometimes I don't understand him.

QUESTION: WHY WOULD ANCIENT AZTECS BE GOING TO THE MOVIES? ANSWER: FORTHCOMING!

ALWAYS WEAR PANTS. ALWAYS WEAR YOUR WINGS. AND DON'T FALL FOR CARMELITA.

THE DISPOSABLE ROADSTER

CARMELITA'S DAD REALLY INVENTS SOME BOSS STUFF! CHECK IT OUT!

THE INFLATABLE PLANE

YAAAHHHH!!!! SIDEKICKS DON'T KISS! YOU'RE SO... YOU'RE SO NOT ARTHUR! YOU DRESS LIKE ARTHUR. OH, YEAH, YOU'RE SOFT, LIKE ARTHUR. BUT YOU CURVE IN ALL THE WRONG PLACES!

SUN WOR-SHIPING DOG LAUNCHERS! YOU FACE THE TICK! AND HIS DOG, SPEAK!

MIDNIGHT BOMBER SEZ: "HE SAYS TO ME, 'YOU GOTTA DO SOMETHING SMART, BABY! SOMETHING BIG!'"

132 HA

MIGHTY BLUE JUSTICE!

Discover the amazing and ancient world of the Aztecs. All their secrets are found within these very pages... **FOR THE VERY FIRST TIME!!!** Marvel at startling facts! The Aztecs were loyal sun worshipers! They used chocolate beans for money! They built breathtaking pyramids, without the help of the Egyptians! They could cause the sun to eclipse by using the power of their minds! They kept fire-breathing monkeys as pets! Their world had all this - and **MUCH MUCH MORE!!!**

It's all here in this latest book by noted author **Aha Mazolama**, writer of the critically acclaimed *Lost World of the French!*, *Mysterious Denmark!*, and *Microwave Cooking Made Super Easy!*

Aztecs On My Mind

NOW IN PAPERBACK

AZTECS ON MY MIND

I JUST FOUND OUT THAT SPEAK IS NOT A DOG. HE'S A CAPYBARA, ONE OF THE WORLD'S LARGEST RODENTS!

MY DOG SPEAK
BY THE TICK
LOOK AT MY DOG! I NAMED HIM SPEAK. MY DOG SPEAK CAN REALLY SPEAK. MY DOG IS THE BEST! I LOVE MY DOG SPEAK.

WELL, I HOPE YOU BOYS HAVE LEARNED YOUR LESSON. IN LOVE, THERE'S A RIGHT WAY AND A WRONG WAY TO DO THINGS. THE RIGHT WAY IS TO TAKE SOMEONE TO A MOVIE. THE WRONG WAY IS TO TAKE SOMEONE FROM A MOVIE. BECAUSE KIDNAPPING IS JUST PLAIN WRONG! NOT ONLY THAT, IT'S WRONG IN THE EYES OF THE LAW. WALLY, I'M PRETTY SURE THEY'LL TRY YOU AS AN ADULT. I'M NOT TALKING ABOUT DETENTION, NEITHER; I'M TALKING ABOUT DETENTION! AND WHAT HAVE WE LEARNED ABOUT AZTECS? WELL, NOTHING REALLY. BECAUSE YOU CAN'T TRUST EVERYTHING YOU READ, ESPECIALLY IN HISTORY BOOKS YOU GET IN GAS STATIONS. BUT YOU CAN TRUST SPEAK! RIGHT, BOY?

THE TICK'S STUFF

133
HA

Arthur's Casebook

While I was working on my new diet, and Tick was...trying...to train Speak, we got an urgent call from Four-Legged Man. The Civic Minded Five were battling a villain who called himself Baron Violent, and they needed our help. The Tick saw this as an opportunity for Speak's first adventure. I wasn't so sure that this was a good idea, but once The Tick gets an idea planted in his head, there's no stopping him. While Tick took on Baron Violent, the Civic Minded Five told me that Violent's belt was the source of his strength. The Tick's mind wasn't entirely on the battle, because he was looking out for Speak. I went for Baron Violent's belt and "turned him off." He was just a little scrawny guy, who ran away crying when I wouldn't give him his belt back. We then decided that Tick should take Speak to see the vet (finally!). I went home with Baron Violent's belt, and decided to try it out. It worked. It gave me the physique of The Tick...and better, even. And it felt good. I called up Carmelita, to take her out to dinner. At dinner, two thugs started picking on me. The "old Arthur" would have been frightened, but with me as the "new Arthur," it was easy to take care of these two. I then spotted the puny Baron Violent and turned up the belt. I got even bigger. I loved it! I told that little dipstick to get out of my city! Carmelita took off on me, but who cares? Who needs her, anyway?

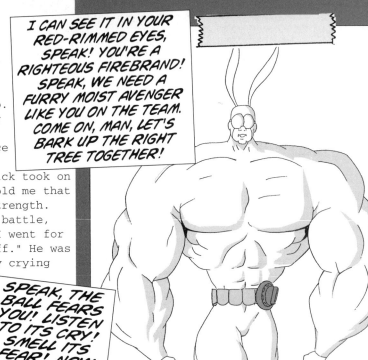

I CAN SEE IT IN YOUR RED-RIMMED EYES, SPEAK! YOU'RE A RIGHTEOUS FIREBRAND! SPEAK, WE NEED A FURRY MOIST AVENGER LIKE YOU ON THE TEAM. COME ON, MAN, LET'S BARK UP THE RIGHT TREE TOGETHER!

SPEAK, THE BALL FEARS YOU! LISTEN TO ITS CRY! SMELL ITS FEAR! NOW FETCH!

Carmelita's Diary

Arthur changed into a big, superstrong idiot. I figured our only chance to help him was to get The Tick. I took The Tick back to the restaurant, where Arthur was being a terrible jerk. We pleaded with him to give over the belt, but he wouldn't do it. Arthur and The Tick struggled, and Arthur grew even bigger. He took me and ran off to the top of a building. The Tick followed, and Arthur attacked him and the almost fell over the side of the building. The Tick held on to the roof and grabbed Arthur by his ears, but the only way he could save Arthur was to ahve him turn down his muscles. Unfortunately, his arms were so huge that he couldn't reach the belt. The ears tore, and I was his only hope. I flew down and turned the belt off, returning Arthur to his normal shape and size. Arthur knew how horrible he had been, and threw off the belt and destroyed it. The next day The Tick, Arthur, and I spent the day fixing up the Bistro D'Burden.

Arthur's Casebook - Addendum

I realized what a jerk I had been, and I wanted Tick and Carmelita to know that I was really, really sorry.

934 HA

I'M TAKING OFF THE KID GLOVES, AND PUTTING ON THE VERY MAD GLOVES!

MIGHTY BLUE JUSTICE!

TROPICAL PARASITES, YOUR CAREFREE INFESTATION ENDS HERE! TONIGHT, YOU SWIM IN OINTMENTS OF RIGHTEOUS HYGIENE. FLEE BEFORE THE MIGHT OF MODERN MEDICINE! MITES, LICE, AND CHIGGERS, YOUR DAYS ARE NUMBERED. YES, IN THIS HOUSE, CLEANLINESS IS NEXT TO DOGLINESS! OH, SPEAK! I'M SORRY, I DIDN'T MEAN IT. OF COURSE, YOU'RE NOT A DOG, YOU'RE A WONDERFUL, LOVELY RODENT. AND THERE'S NOTHING WRONG WITH THAT. NO! AND IF THAT'S YOUR LIFESTYLE CHOICE, THEN WE'LL STAND BEHIND YOU ALL THE WAY.

Dr. Sniff, V.M.D.
ANIMAL HOSPITAL

Patient: **Speak**
Owner: **The Tick**

    Speak suffers from a mild case of eczema, worms, and the mange. Apply ointment twice daily to remedy.
    Speak is not a dog. He is a *Hydrochaerus hydrochaeris*. Or more commonly known as a Capybara, one of the world's largest rodents.

LET YOUR JOURNEY INTO HUGENESS TEACH US ALL A LESSON. ABSOLUTE POWER IS A STICKY WICKET. AND, ARTHUR, CHUM, YOU WERE THE STICKIEST. DON'T YOU GET IT, GOOD FRIEND? SOME OF THE BEST THINGS COME IN SMALL PACKAGES. BUT LARGE THINGS CAN'T! UNLESS THEY'RE INFLATABLE, OR REQUIRE SOME ASSEMBLY, OR UNLESS THEY'RE HEARTS! YES, GIANT, JUICY, LOVING HEARTS! AS BIG AS THE MOON, BUT MUCH, MUCH WARMER! RIGHT, SPEAK?

Arthur's Casebook

The Tick found a ~~Mr. Mental~~ baby left at our door. We had to take him in and raise him. Yes, that's what we had to do. We took the ~~Mr. Mental~~ baby to the park to play with the ~~Mr. Mental~~ baby. There, the worst possible thing happened; the ~~Mr. Mental~~ baby was attacked by dingoes! We fought off the dingoes, who could talk, and some of them turned into men. They fled, but we lost the ~~Mr. Mental~~ baby. I found the ~~Mr. Mental~~ baby, but... he... frightened me, and (I think) told me to leave him alone. We went home, and the ~~Mr. Mental~~ baby's mother came by to drop off a toy. She also said his ~~Mr. Mental's~~ name was Mel. After ~~Mr. Mental~~ Mel got his toy, he locked himself in the bedroom. I looked through the keyhole to see what ~~Mr. Mental~~ Mel was doing and he ...frightened... me again. But just then, I figured out that this ~~Mr. Mental~~ baby was really the master criminal MR. MENTHOL(?), or rather MR. MENTAL! Mr. Mental, used the device/toy he was making to create a mental energy monster that smashed though my ceiling and grabbed The Tick. It was up to me to sever the cord from Mr. Mental's mind to the monster. I had to bite through it! Ick!

ARTHUR! WE'RE A DADDY!

POPPA'S GOT A BRAND-NEW BAG... OF FISH!

NOBODY MAULS THE TICK'S SIDEKICK. AND NOBODY TOUCHES THE TICK'S BABY! EVER!

WELL, MEL MENTAL, I CAN FORGIVE YOU FOR TRYING TO TAKE OVER THE WORLD, BUT NOT FOR STEALING MY HEART! DAYS FROM NOW, ARTHUR AND I WILL LOOK AROUND OUR EMPTY APARTMENT AND WONDER, "WHERE'S BABY? WHERE'S OUR LITTLE BUNDLE OF JOY?" AND HE'LL BE IN PRISON! HOW COULD YOU DO THIS TO US? YOU MADE A MOCKERY OF EVERYTHING THIS FAMILY STOOD FOR!

EVERYBODY WAS A BABY ONCE, ARTHUR. OH, SURE, MAYBE NOT TODAY, OR EVEN YESTERDAY. BUT ONCE! BABIES, CHUM: TINY, DIMPLED, FLESHY LITTLE MIRRORS OF OUR US-NESS, THAT WE PARENTS HURL INTO THE FUTURE, LIKE LEATHERY FOOTBALLS OF HOPE! AND YOU'VE GOT TO GET A GOOD SPIRAL ON THAT BABY, OR EVIL WILL MAKE AN INTERCEPTION!

Please take care of my dear sweet child. I know you are good kind men who can protect him from a cruel world filled with bad things

Signed,
The ~~Baby~~ Mother

Dingoes Stole My Baby!

136

HA

MIGHTY BLUE JUSTI

SEWER URCHIN'S "BATTLE GEAR"

HEAVY COMBAT

ARCTIC SEWER

AH HA-HA, CHESS! THE ANCIENT CONTEST OF WITS. TWO OPPONENTS: MANO E MANO. BRAINO E BRAINO. AND LOOK! MAGNETS FOR EASE OF TRAVEL! YOU COULD PLAY CHESS ON THE MOON!

SEWERS OF PARIS

WHAT WAS THAT WITH THE LOBSTERS? I THOUGHT THERE WERE ALLIGATORS IN THE SEWERS. I WAS READY FOR ALLIGATORS.

LOOK! BOSS HELMETS FOR US!

WE'RE SWORN TO PROTECT THE CITY. AND WE'RE JUST GOING TO HAVE TO FACE IT, AND THAT INCLUDES THE SEWERS.

THE TICK'S STUFF

Arthur's Casebook

Tick, Die Fledermaus, and Sewer Urchin were sitting around the diner playing chess, when the most stunning thing happened: A group of municipal employees came requesting help from Sewer Urchin. Urchin immediately rushed to their aid, and Tick and I followed. Urchin warned us that his mission would be difficult and dangerous, but we could come if we could keep up. We first went to Sewer Urchin's headquarters, which was amazing! We then traveled on through the Sewers, and Urchin told us that the terrible threat came from a man calling himself SewerCzar, the Czar of the Sewers, and he needed to be stopped before he could carry out his plans of revenge upon The City. Sewer Urchin led us on a quest to SewerCzar's base where we (well, actually, Tick) stumbled into the traps and threats of Sewer Lobsters and Wallet Anglers. Then Sewer Urchin realized that we were surrounded by Filth. He had us lather up with soap for protection. We fought them off, and figured that was it. Mission over! But no, Sewer Urchin said this was just the beginning. Suddenly, we found ourselves in a tunnel that was flooded with water. Sewer Urchin managed to save us, but fell into a trap full of Sewer Lobsters. We lost Sewer Urchin and wound up in SewerCzar's hideout, and in a vat of unprossessed Filth. Then, to out great surprise, Sewer Urchin showed up, having fought off the lobster menace. Then the Filth, decided that they liked Urchin's theories of waste management better then SewerCzar's and turned against him, resulting in his defeat. After this whole adventure, both Tick and I had a new respect for Sewer Urchin!

DANGERS OF THE SEWERS

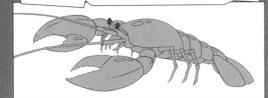

The sewers are a mighty dangerous place, full of horrible traps ready to mess you up (in more ways than one!).

Sewer Lobsters: That's right, lobsters. Most people think that the sewers are crawling with alligators (I know I did!), but they're not! They're crawling with lobsters. Ever seen a lobster in a restaurant? See those elastic bands on their claws? Those bands are there for a reason! Sewer Lobsters pinch really hard! If you are attacked by Sewer Lobsters, a little melted butter and lemon will chase them away.

Wallet Angler: A horrible fish monster that uses a living wallet for bait! So if you see what looks like a lost wallet laying there, don't try to pick it up, because that's just what the Wallet Angler's want! He'll scoop you up and make you his lunch! I know it's tempting to pick up a lost wallet and try to help someone out, but resist the temptation to help when traveling the sewers.

Filth: Filth are the monster henchmen of SewerCzar. If you come acoss Filth, just get out of there! Seek out a superhero immediately! Sewer Urchin would be your best choice. Honest.

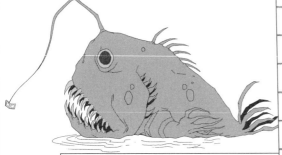

WE SPENT ALL NIGHT LEARNING AN IMPORTANT LESSON: YOU CAN'T JUDEGE A SEWER BY ITS MANHOLE COVER. NO SIR, PEOPLE CAN BE VERY DIFFERENT UNDER THE SURFACE THAN THEY MIGHT SEEM. QUIET, MILD-MANNERED SOULS JUST MIGHT TURN OUT TO BE ROARING LIONS OF TWO-FISTED COOL. AND ROARING LIONS OF TWO-FISTED COOL JUST MIGHT HAVE SOME CRIPPLING LOBSTER PROBLEMS. LISTEN, MAN, IT'S ALL CRAZY DOWN THERE, UNDER THE SURFACE. A LOST WALLET COULD BITE YOU IN HALF! A BAR OF SOAP COULD SAVE YOUR LIFE! EGAD! A DISGUSTING MOUND OF MUCK JUST MIGHT HAVE SOME VERY COMPELLING IDEAS. DO YOU DIG MY DITCH?

DOWN HERE I'M CONSIDIERED THE APOTHEOSIS OF COOL.

936 HA

MIGHTY BLUE JUSTICE

International Superhero Exchange Program

Dear Tick,

Congratulations! You have been chosen to participate in the International Superhero Exchange Program. You will be going to Antwerp, Belgium. We hope that you find this exchange and travel experience an enriching part of your impressive superhero career.

Bon Voyage,

Chief Administrator
I.S.H.E.P.

Here's just a little taste of what's to come. Signed, An old friend.

SPECIAL DELIVERY! OH, ARTHUR! THE THRILL OF MODERN POSTISM!

MY FIRST DAY ON THE CONTINENT, AND ALREADY I HAVE AN ARCHENEMY!

MAJESTY SNATCHERS! UNHAND THAT HIGHNESS!

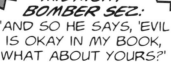

MIDNIGHT BOMBER SEZ: "AND SO HE SAYS, 'EVIL IS OKAY IN MY BOOK, WHAT ABOUT YOURS?' AND I GO, 'YEAH BABY YEAH YEAH!!'"

Arthur's Casebook

The Tick recieved a letter informing him that he had been chosen to participate in the International Superhero Exchange Program. He would spend a month in Antwerp, Belgium, and a Belgian superhero would be sent here to replace him. While Tick got a nice letter, I got a box of cookies which turned out to be evil gingerbread men that ran amok in the apartment. Anyway, I didn't think that this was the best time for Tick to leave, but he said things would be fine. His replacement turned out to be a really amazing superheroine, Eclaire. She proved to be a great ally in the cookie fight back at the apartment, and after a while the gingerbread men all went stale and stopped moving around and being bad. We all realized that the Breadmaster was behind all this when he sent us a letter saying so. He then attacked The City with a glazed gingerbread tank that fired quick-setting frosting. Eclaire got trapped in the frosting, so I went and got some milk, because, you know, milk beats cookies. I threw the milk at the tank's treads, which desolved, and then Eclaire blew up the tank with her eye beams. I wonder if Belgium misses Eclaire?

LET'S JUST SEE HOW YOU FAIR AGAINST TWO-BITS OF FLAT, SHINY AMERICA!

THE TICK'S STUFF

Dear Tick,

Europe must be great. Back here things are okay. Eclaire is a gracious guest, and a powerful force for goodness. Every morning she makes delicious Belgian waffles. Yum yum. But, oh, those gingerbread men. They are some tough, ruthless cookies. Nighttime is the worst. It turns out all of the other super-heroes have gotten them, too. Die Fledermaus says he hasn't slept in a week.
Best Wishes,
Arthur

DEAR ARTHUR,
    HAVING A WONDERFUL TIME. WISH YOU WERE HERE. BELGIANS ARE A POLITE BUT MYSTERIOUS PEOPLE. I'VE BEEN HARDLY SCOLDED FOR MY NORMAL MODE OF TRAVEL. THESE EUROPEANS CAN GET PRETTY TOUCHY ABOUT THIER ARCHITECTURAL TREASURES. NOW I DO MOST OF MY PATROLLING ON THE BACK OF BLITZEN'S MOTORCYCLE. EACH MORNING STARTS AT THE CAFÉ, WITH A LEISURELY CREME COFFEE, A DELIGHTFUL LITTLE CROISSANT ROLL, AND A LOOK AT THE DAY'S NEWS. THEN, IT'S OFF TO SCOUR THE UNDERWORLD, PRESSING FOR LEADS ON THE KIDNAPPED KING. AFTER A HEARTY LUNCH, IT'S TIME FOR AN AFTERNOON SIESTA. THEN WE DANCE TILL DAWN AT ANTWERP'S HOTTEST NIGHT SPOTS!
SIGNED,
TICK

Port of Antwerp as seen at night.

ANTWERP
L7T

42f

ARTHUR

NOW I HATE YOU!

ALL RIGHT! I BOUGHT HIS BRAIN!

WHEN A NICE CLEAN BRAIN TUMBLES TO THE DIRTY STREET TO LAY AMONG THE DISCARDED WRAPPERS AND SPAT OUT GUM WADS OF WICKEDNESS, YOU CAN'T JUST PICK IT UP AND WASH IT OFF WITH SOAP AND WATER; YOU HAVE TO THINK IT CLEAN FROM THE INSIDE OUT!

146

HA

MIGHTY BLUE JUSTICE!

LETTERS TO THE TICK

As a well-known and beloved superhero, I receive a lot of mail from admirers and well-wishers. Also, a good percentage of my so-called "fan mail" comes from America's lovable little moppets, those ever curious citizens we call children. Some of these fine youngsters, who look up to me, both figuratively and literally, ask me questions. Questions so insightful and important, I MUST ANSWER THEM! Now here, for one and all, are some of the questions with the important answers provided by me! Let the insight begin!

Dear Tick,
       What would you do if bees took over the world?
—Hogarth Laemle
age 6

What would I do?! EGAD, HOGARTH! I would conform! When the bees implement their worldwide fascist regime, I will be the first to go down into the honey mines! I will be the first to carry their squirming larvae in my teeth! The first to smear ROYAL JELLY on their CHOSEN QUEEN! And why? GOOD HEAVENS, ON ACCOUNT OF THE STINGING!

THE TICK'S STUFF

Dear Tick,

Why do parents always tell us what to do, but never ask how we feel?
—Beth Fury
age 11

Grown-ups, Beth Fury, are a strange breed! Their brains weigh close to three pounds, and that's not three pounds of cheery delight, no! ~~That's three pounds of day-job and time-clockery, three pounds of the~~ terror and anguish that is the permanent emergency of child rearing! The fact that a grown-up can take charge of anything is KNOCK- ~~DOWN-DRAG-OUT AMAZING! THINK HOW THEY FEEL!~~

Dear Tick,

Why does my grandmother always have to pinch my cheeks?
—Naomi Shingle
age 9

NAOMI SHINGLE! Think like a grand- mother! You're there, you're a person, and then suddenly, through the miracle of life, you have a child! Years pass, and then that child grows up and has a child of its own: you, Naomi Shingle! Your grandmother is one of the strongest, old- est links in that great chain of being we call humanity and that's gotta be ~~PRETTY BOSS! It's a wonder she isn't pinching everything in sight!~~

Dear Tick,

If carp were flying backwards in Spain, and pandas were doing handstands in the deserts of China, how much rain would my town get?
—Keel Stoker
age 12

This letter is clearly the result of too much spinning! KEEL STOKER! I know chil- dren love to spin, round and round on the emerald lawns of Anytown, USA! Goodness knows, I love a good spin myself! But you've got to know when to stop, boy! ~~You're spinning your tyke melon into a kaleidoscope of crazy! I say~~ to you: Spinning and writing letters don't mix!

MIDNIGHT BOMBER SEZ:
"AND SO HE SAYS, 'I DON'T LIKE THE CUT OF YOUR JIB!' AND I GO, 'IT'S THE ONLY JIB I GOT, BABY!!!'"

142
HA
MIGHTY BLUE JUSTICE

Dear Tick,

Why do trees grow upwards? And what can we do to save the trees?
—Tammi Figg
age 11

Trees, beautiful trees! Those big, stiff flowers of the forest. Why, they grow all kinds of ways! "Up" is just the one we notice the most! Their roots grow downwards into rich earth, and their branches grow sideways to... to... TO MINGLE! Now, what can Tammi Figg do to help save the trees? Well, number one: STOP WRITING LETTERS! They're made of TREES!

MIDNIGHT BOMBER SEZ: "EAT MY SMOKE, COPPER!"

Dear Tick,

What makes us ticklish?
—Helmut Fitzgerald
age 26

It's not that we are ticklish, as much as our skin is ticklish. So, what's with skin? SKIN! TEN LAYERS THICK AND DYING ON TOP! SKIN! The largest organ our bodies have to offer — and those who tickle the ivories of that organ are playing the oldest song in the body's book. Don't you see? That's why the child's laughter is so much like music, and that's why people are ticklish, Helmut. Because people need to laugh — AND CLOWNS JUST DON'T CUT IT!

Dear Tick,

Why are boys always mean to girls?
—Fiona Zimmer
age 8

The body of an average boy is a strange battleground. A volcanic mess of snakes, snails, and puppy dog tails. Meanness breeds like mosquito larvae in their derelict kiddie-pool hearts. I understand, Fiona! Why, indeed! GIRLS OF THE WORLD, UNITE AND TAKE OVER! GROOVY ALL-FEMALE WORLD NOW!!!

Dear Tick,

How many stars are there in the universe?
—Weiss Corkey
age 41

I am told, by preeminent counting experts, that there are as many stars in the universe as there are grains of sand on a beach. This may seem confusing, at first, but not when you consider the many works of that evenhanded minx we call symmetry! Look around, Weiss Corkey! All kinds of things are symmetrical: horses, prom dresses, hydrogen molecules — why, even YOU! And where there's symmetry, there's lots of other stuff...

149

THE TICK'S STUFF

Dear Tick,
       Who would win in a fight, you or Dracula?
—Clay Chisolm
age 13

Okay, Clay. I'll play your little game for a moment. Let's see... Dracula certainly has the wisdom of centuries on his side, he commands all the dark power of FULL-ON CREEPY, and he looks good in velvet. But I am mighty, and a good heart is worth ten Draculas in the light of day! Plus, Dracula is a fictional character, whereas I am real—and real beats made-up every time!

Dear Tick,
       How come every time someone asks you a question, you never really answer it? All you do is jibber-jabber.
—Amy Lanza
age 11

Jibber-jabber?! Oh, Amy Lanza, you cut me to the quickest! What can I possibly say to... JIBBER-JABBER!? Heavens to Mergatroid! I'm no public speaker, I am a frothing fount of pure common sensitivity! I can no more structure my response to a given question than I could stem the tide of a mighty river, or stunt the feet of a tiny empress. JIBBER-JABBER! What's so bad about jibber-jabber? What's the next thing the Amy Lanzas of the world will outlaw? Kindness?

SPOON!

MIGHTY BLUE JUSTICE!

PART 6: STUFF AT THE END OF THE BOOK

Some might call this something really highbrow, like an "Index," but I just call it somewhere to help you look stuff up in this book, and make it so you can find it really fast! If you are faced by a rampaging Proto-Clown, and can't remember if he likes to be laughed at or not, then time is definitely NOT on your side!

MIDNIGHT BOMBER SEZ:
"AND THEN I SAYS, 'TELL ME I'M WRONG!' AND HE SAYS, 'I CAN'T BABY! CAUSE YOU'RE NOT!!!'"

MIDNIGHT BOMBER SEZ: "ONE OF THESE DAYS... MILKSHAKE! BOOM!"

STUFF AT THE END OF THE BOOK 147

STUFF AT THE END OF THE BOOK 149